"Most of us struggle with what to say an[d do] with a person who is grieving. This wond[erful book helps us feel] comfortable ministering after a death b[y showing us] what your family member or friend needs most. I read this book on an airplane, headed for a funeral. I learned helpful things that I was able to use immediately."

Steve Grissom, Founder, GriefShare

"Grief persists as a constant presence in a fallen world. And as common as grief is, so is the silence of friends or family members who aren't quite sure how to help. Nancy Guthrie's *What Grieving People Wish You Knew* enters into this silent void and offers the clear and practical voice of experience and wisdom. In a unique and captivating way, Guthrie unleashes the testimonies of numerous individuals who have recently experienced grief. Their words, along with Guthrie's synthesis, allow the reader to know what truly helps and what truly hurts as we seek to minister to our grief-stricken loved ones. Do you want to be a good friend to those grieving around you? Then this is the book for you."

Jason Helopoulos, Associate Pastor, University Reformed Church, East Lansing, Michigan; author, *A Neglected Grace: Family Worship in the Christian Home*

"Someday, someone close to each of us will die. During that difficult time, the right words can comfort us and point us to Christ. *What Grieving People Wish You Knew* offers great counsel from those who went through the dark days of a loved one's death. For friends of the grieving, this book can help you to offer comfort. In this book are examples of healing words that grievers need to hear—told by those who longed to hear them. These stories from those of us who have grieved, and are still grieving, will give believers the confidence to come and sit with us on the mourning bench."

Mark Green, President, *The White Horse Inn*

"*What Grieving People Wish You Knew* is a timely and priceless resource for men and women who are compelled to live out the Bible's directive to 'weep with those who weep' but feel helpless to do so. This book is profoundly practical, and I am personally grateful to have it as a resource to share with so many who desire to love the grieving well."

Raechel Myers, cofounder, She Reads Truth

"Nancy Guthrie writes pointedly about trying to minister to hurting people. We can all learn much from poor examples—from Job's miserable comforters. *What Grieving People Wish You Knew* provides an A+ lesson plan in what not to say and do as comforters. Of course, Nancy does not stop there, for she also writes poignantly about Christlike comfort. With wisdom and compassion, Nancy weaves Scripture, her story, and the stories of scores of grievers to encourage, empower, and equip us to esteem grief and to care like Christ as we minister to those who grieve."

Bob Kellemen, Biblical Counseling Chair, Crossroads Bible College; author, *God's Healing for Life's Losses: How to Find Hope When You're Hurting*

"This book is tender, compassionate, clear, honest, gospel-rich, and practical. There is nothing distant and theoretical about it, because it's written out of the deep well of the author's own experience. I now know what I will give to everyone God sends my way who is suffering loss."

Paul David Tripp, President, Paul Tripp Ministries; author, *New Morning Mercies*

"In the aftermath of deep loss, grievers struggle to articulate what is helpful. These honest and practical suggestions will equip tenderhearted people to come alongside us as we grieve."

Kay Warren, cofounder, Saddleback Church; international speaker; best-selling author, *Choose Joy*

What Grieving People Wish You Knew

about What Really Helps

(and What Really Hurts)

WHAT GRIEVING PEOPLE

WISH YOU KNEW

about What Really Helps

(and What Really Hurts)

Nancy Guthrie

:: CROSSWAY®

WHEATON, ILLINOIS

What Grieving People Wish You Knew about What Really Helps (and What Really Hurts)
Copyright © 2016 by Nancy Guthrie
Published by Crossway
1300 Crescent Street
Wheaton, Illinois 60187

Cover design: Josh Dennis

First printing 2016

Printed in the United States of America

Unless otherwise indicated, Scripture quotations are from the ESV® Bible (The Holy Bible, English Standard Version®), copyright © 2001 by Crossway, a publishing ministry of Good News Publishers. Used by permission. All rights reserved.

Scripture quotations marked HCSB have been taken from *The Holman Christian Standard Bible®*. Copyright © 1999, 2000, 2002, 2003 by Holman Bible Publishers. Used by permission.

Scripture quotations marked KJV are from the *King James Version* of the Bible.

Scripture quotations marked MESSAGE are from *The Message*. Copyright © by Eugene H. Peterson 1993, 1994, 1995, 1996, 2000, 2001, 2002. Used by permission of NavPress Publishing Group.

Scripture quotations marked NASB are from *The New American Standard Bible®*. Copyright © The Lockman Foundation 1960, 1962, 1963, 1968, 1971, 1972, 1973, 1975, 1977, 1995. Used by permission.

Scripture quotations marked NET are from *The NET Bible®* copyright © 2003 by Biblical Studies Press, L.L.C. www.netbible.com. All rights reserved. Quoted by permission.

Scripture references marked NIV are taken from The Holy Bible, New International Version®, NIV®. Copyright © 1973, 1978, 1984, 2011 by Biblica, Inc.™ Used by permission. All rights reserved worldwide.

Scripture references marked NLT are from *The Holy Bible, New Living Translation*, copyright © 1996, 2004. Used by permission of Tyndale House Publishers, Inc., Wheaton, IL, 60189. All rights reserved.

All emphases in scripture quotations have been added by the author.

Trade paperback ISBN: 978-1-4335-5235-9
ePub ISBN: 978-1-4335-5238-0
PDF ISBN: 978-1-4335-5236-6
Mobipocket ISBN: 978-1-4335-5237-3

Library of Congress Cataloging-in-Publication Data

Names: Guthrie, Nancy, author.
Title: What grieving people wish you knew about what really helps (and what really hurts) / Nancy Guthrie.
Description: Wheaton : Crossway, 2016. | Includes bibliographical references and index.
Identifiers: LCCN 2016017699 (print) | LCCN 2016025890 (ebook) | ISBN 9781433552359 (tp) | ISBN 9781433552366 (pdf) | ISBN 9781433552373 (mobi) | ISBN 9781433552380 (epub)
Subjects: LCSH: Bereavement--Religious aspects--Christianity. | Grief—Religious aspects—Christianity. | Consolation.
Classification: LCC BV4905.3 .G89 2016 (print) | LCC BV4905.3 (ebook) | DDC 248.8/66—dc23
LC record available at https://lccn.loc.gov/2016017699

Crossway is a publishing ministry of Good News Publishers.

BP		26	25	24	23	22	21	20	19	18
15	14	13	12	11	10	9	8	7	6	5	4	3

With admiration and appreciation, I dedicate this book to the thousands of GriefShare facilitators in churches around the country who, week by week, meet with grieving people who are trying to navigate their way through the hardest and darkest place they've ever been. Each of you could write a book like this yourself, because you have heard so many people lament the sorrow that was added to their sorrow by those who didn't know better, as well as the comfort provided by those who had the courage to reach out. Thank you for listening to their stories, giving them a safe place to voice their lingering questions, painful regrets, and aching loneliness, even as you point them toward the healing to be found in Christ.

Contents

Introduction

I have to tell you something up front: I think you're awesome. I assume you're reading this book or considering reading this book because you want to figure out how you can be a better friend to people around you who are going through the devastation of losing someone they love. You want to be better equipped for the awkward interactions. You don't want to be that person who said the stupid, hurtful thing. Instead you want to grow in your ability to come alongside someone who is hurting and enter in. So I applaud you for being willing to invest in finding out more about what that looks and sounds like.

To be honest, I didn't think much about grief or grieving people for most of my life. I didn't have to. Or, what is, perhaps, more deeply true, is that I didn't choose to. I suppose I operated with a convenient naiveté about the deep sorrow and social awkwardness people experience when someone they love dies. But once you've been there, it is more difficult to keep an unaffected distance from people in your world who have lost someone and are wondering how the world around them could just keep on turning as if nothing has changed, since it feels as if their world has collapsed.

Grief barged through the doors of our lives uninvited on

November 24, 1998. That was the day a geneticist who had just examined our two-day-old daughter, Hope, came to my hospital room and told my husband, David, and me that he suspected Hope had a rare metabolic disorder called Zellweger syndrome. This meant that all of her cells were missing a tiny sub-cellular particle called "peroxisomes" that rids the cells of toxins. A great deal of damage had already been done to all of her major organs—especially her liver, kidneys, and brain. He told us there was no treatment or cure and that most children with the syndrome live less than six months.

A few days later, when we took her home from the hospital, we knew we were taking her home to die. The 199 days that she was with us were rich in many ways. We did the best we could to pack as much living and loving in those days as we could. And then we said good-bye.

Initially, in those days after she died, I felt full and enriched from all we had experienced with her and wise from all we had learned in our experience with her. But that faded quickly. A load of sadness settled in that felt like a boulder on my chest so that I was always struggling to catch my breath.

For a child to have this syndrome means that David and I have to be carriers of the recessive gene trait for it, so any child of ours has a 25 percent chance of having the fatal syndrome. So we took surgical steps to prevent another pregnancy. And evidently it didn't work. A year and a half after Hope died, I discovered I was pregnant. Prenatal tests revealed this child, a son, also had the fatal syndrome. So we welcomed our son Gabriel in July 2001. He, too, was with us about six months. And there we were again—David; our son, Matt; and me—in a very quiet house, working our way separately but together through sadness.

Over these years since Hope and Gabriel died, I've inter-acted with many grieving people. I've listened to grieving people talk about their deep disappointment and ongoing alienation from people around them who just don't seem to "get it." But I've also heard them speak movingly of the unexpected, often simple things people around them have said or done that dem-onstrated a deep sensitivity to their pain and a willingness to enter into it with them.

It's easy to sit with grieving people and swap stories about ridiculous, thoughtless, insensitive things people around them have said and done. Too easy, perhaps. What is much sweeter and certainly more helpful is to talk about what people have said or done that touched them deeply, what was especially meaningful and helped them not feel so alone in the midst of sorrow. So that's what I asked people to do. I asked them, via an online survey posted on various websites, to tell me what others said or did for them that was especially helpful or meaningful in the midst of grief. I asked them what they wish those around them had understood about their grief. I heard from people of all ages and situations who have experienced all kinds of losses. And I've incorporated what these grieving people told me throughout this book.

In fact, I've just got to share a few things people told me here at the outset so that you'll have a taste of what's ahead. If you doubt that you have any power to bring comfort to someone going through unimaginable loss, surely these will convince you otherwise:

When my grandmother passed away from dementia, someone wrote, "I'm so sorry you didn't get to say good-bye the way you wanted to." It still brings tears to my eyes that someone said exactly what I didn't even know how to express.

Emily McKillip, Fort Worth, Texas

Almost a year after our infant son was born dead, a woman at church talked about him, using his name in a conversation, and I almost wept with gratitude! I didn't realize how much it hurt that everyone tried not to talk about him to protect me from further pain, when really the most pain was from others dodging his existence at every turn.

Lindsey Coffman, Milford, Kansas

In the hospital cafeteria one day with my pastor, I said, "I'm not sure I can hold on to God through this." He answered, "You can't hold on to him, but he will hold on to you." That gave me such comfort—knowing I could just let God hold on to me, and he has.

Judy Joyce, Richmond, Virginia

After my husband died, a friend invited me to stay with her and her husband for a while in a little cottage in their backyard. I had space to be alone when I couldn't handle social situations, but they were nearby if I needed to talk.

Carol Miller, Waverly, New York

My husband and I were in our doctor's office waiting room a few months after our thirty-four-year-old son died. An acquaintance whose son had played basketball with our son worked there. She glanced at us from the back of the office and could have easily looked away. Instead, she got up from her desk, walked out and around through several doors, and came up to us. She said, "I am sorry to do this here, but this has to be acknowledged." She tenderly hugged each of us in the middle of the waiting room. I had some tears, but it touched my soul.

Jan Kelley, Wichita, Kansas

The morning after our son passed, as I rose dreading another day, there was our elderly new neighbor, meticulously sweeping our sidewalk. He never looked up; he just swept and went on his way. I will never forget that singular, anonymous act of kindness.

GriefShare facilitator, Tampa Bay, Florida

My wife and I had tried for about seven years to get pregnant, which was its own monthly agony. Then we got pregnant and announced it to our church friends, and we all rejoiced. Then we miscarried, and we were devastated, as were our friends. The one caring comment that I've never forgotten came from a man who never talked much. He looked me right in the eye, with tears in his, and said he knew that some people might try to comfort us with the thought that because the miscarriage happened early, it would hurt less. Then he said, "As soon as you knew you were pregnant, you were in love with that baby." He said he knew how much we must be hurting, and he was sorry. I've never forgotten that brief conversation. I'm tearing up as I write this, more than twenty-five years later.

David J. Myers, Caldwell, Idaho

After our son drowned, a friend called me up and said, "I am going to make us hair appointments for the same time so I can take you." When she called ahead, she told our hairdresser what had happened so she would not start asking me about the kids.

Rachel Anderson, College Station, Texas

Six months after losing our baby, we went to a wedding. As we were leaving the party, the couple asked if they could leave a bouquet of their wedding flowers on our daughter's grave. In the midst of their happiest day they remembered our sadness.

Ruth, UK

In the span of three months three of my young friends passed away. The most significant thing someone did for me was to continuously pursue friendship with my tired self. Instead of pitying me from afar, she entered in with compassion. This meant sometimes being able to talk about where I was and how I was coping, but most of the time it meant helping me to see the beauty in life by exploring the city in which we live, going out with girls, trying new coffee shops, etc. Being a friend who drew near in spite of my changing moods and energy levels reminded me that regardless, I was ever loved.

Beth Gowing, Montreal, Quebec, Canada

In my grief I needed to discharge my burden, and I needed someone who was in God's Word and walking in it. I needed seasoned maturity, a loving heart, and all that comes with it. I knew such a person and told her I needed to talk. She sat outside with me on folding chairs between our parked cars for hours on end as I shared my story and my grief. I spoke in linear fashion; she spoke but little, but when she did, it was right and something I could use. The evening came on, but I was not done. After we took care of some things, we found ourselves at a track. We walked around it again and again as I finished my story. Night fell, my burden discharged.

Anonymous

Simple but incredible stuff, don't you think? When I read things like this, I wonder why I ever hesitate to speak up or reach out to someone who is grieving. I wonder why I ever let the temporary awkwardness rob me of the joy and satisfaction of blessing someone in such a significant way during such a difficult time. I hope you feel that way too and that you'll find ideas and encouragement in the pages that follow. I also hope that you will be emboldened to engage instead of avoid the grieving people who are all around you and are waiting for someone to interact with them about the loss of their loved one.

Along with the courage to engage, most of us need some wisdom in regard to what meaningful engagement with grieving people looks and sounds like. So let's dive in. Let's explore together what grieving people wish you knew about what really helps and what really hurts.

1

WHAT TO SAY

(AND WHAT NOT TO SAY)

It was just two months after our daughter, Hope, died. My husband, David, and I found ourselves attending two funerals in one day—one for a baby who had died at birth, and another for a child who had died of the same syndrome our daughter had. I was waiting in line to greet the parents at the first funeral, when it hit me: *I have no idea what to say. Of all people, I should know what to say to these friends.* But I didn't. I had no great wisdom that would answer the questions, no soothing truth that would take away the hurt.

I stumbled through both encounters and walked away with sympathy for all the people who, over the previous months, had struggled to know what to say to David and me. And I went away with more compassion for those who'd felt so helpless that they'd said nothing at all.

Let's face it—it's awkward. We want to say something

personal, something meaningful, beautiful, helpful, sensitive. Something that demonstrates that we have a sense of what they're going through. And what we don't want is to be that person who says the stupid, insensitive thing.

Over many years now of interacting with grieving people— most of whom emerge from their experience of sorrow bent on setting the world straight on what to say and what not to say to people like themselves—I've learned a thing or two that people going through grief wish people understood. I have lots of specific, practical, usable ideas in the pages that follow, but the first and most important thing I have to tell you is this:

It matters less what you say than that you say *something*.

I remember well what a friend who had lost a child told me shortly before Hope died. "It wasn't so much what people said that hurt," she said. "What hurt was when people said nothing at all." All too soon I discovered what she meant; the silence that seemed to scream that my daughter's life didn't even merit a mention. And, oh, how it hurt.

My husband discovered it too on his first day back to work after Hope died. A man came into his office talking a mile a minute but didn't acknowledge our loss at all. David knew he knew. Maybe he thought David wouldn't want to talk about it. Maybe he didn't know how to bring it up. Maybe he thought the office was not the place for it. Most likely he just felt awkward and unsure of what to say, and so he just said nothing. Whatever it was, it hurt.

I also remember well, however, that humbling day when I realized how often I had been that person—that person who said *nothing* about the loss of a loved one to someone stinging with grief. I saw my friend Susan, whose mother had died. I remembered how I had neglected to say anything early on, assuming that since so many other people were speaking to her about her loss, surely she wouldn't notice if I didn't.

What I didn't understand at the time is that when you're grieving, you know who has acknowledged it in some way and who hasn't. You just do.

Saying something about it tells me that you know that it's there, and you care that it's there, and you care about me. Not mentioning it, for whatever reason, makes me feel less cared for by you. In fact, because you choose not to say anything about it, because you choose not to acknowledge it, I find myself doubting whether you care about me at all, because this is the very hardest, biggest thing in my life. If you don't acknowledge it, much less enter into it with me, it puts a huge distance between us.

If I were going through some big happy life change—going to college, or getting married, or having a baby—it would be very strange if you kept refusing to acknowledge it or never wanted to hear anything about it. This grief and loss that I am experiencing are no less life changing.

I don't expect you to know what to say. I'm not asking you to have the answers. In fact, rather than sitting there worrying about what you should say to me, it would be incredible if you would just invite me to share with you. I would feel so loved. But when you don't ask, when you don't bring up this grief, when you so clearly feel uncomfortable with anything vaguely relating to my pain, it makes me feel that my grief is too much for you, that you're not willing to enter into it with me in even the smallest way, and that hurts tremendously.

Jamie Lorenz, Spokane Valley, Washington

Last night I was talking with a friend who was trying to figure out if and how to reach out to someone she hasn't talked to for years who just lost her thirty-five-year-old son. I explained to her that when someone you love has died, it is as if a hurdle has been placed between you and every person you know, and that hurdle stays in place until your loss has been acknowledged in some way. It doesn't have to be a grand gesture or a long conversation. Sometimes a simple, "I know what has happened and I'm so sorry," or even a nonverbal hand on the shoulder or squeeze of the hand will knock down that barrier.

A few months after our daughter died, I was in the carpool line waiting to pick up my son from school, when another mom, who had a daughter born a short time before Hope, came up to my car. She told me that she felt awkward every time she saw me because she still had her daughter while mine was gone, and that she didn't how to get past that awkwardness. "You just did," I told her. Simply acknowledging that the barrier was there knocked it down.

Don't hesitate to approach someone because you think it has been too long since his or her loved one died so that they've probably moved on and wouldn't want to talk about it anymore. The reality is more likely to be the opposite. If it has been a while, it is likely that people have stopped talking about the deceased one, but the grieving one's desire to talk about him or her has only increased. So bring it up. And keep bringing it up over the coming months and even years. That is a gift a true friend gives someone who is grieving.

We love to talk about Savannah, and nothing could be said that would hurt us any more than we were hurting. It actually hurt more when someone didn't say something. Especially when those someones were family members. I think that our presence at family events, just the five of us instead of six, stirred up their grief, and they didn't know what to say or do. It was easier to just stay away, which I interpreted at the time as them not caring or loving Savannah.

Jennifer, Louisiana

I think women do a great job at surrounding one another, encouraging one another, creating a support network. But men, not so much. I can remember one particular Sunday when I stayed home and Peter came home to tell me how many of my friends had asked how I was doing. He was happy about the support I received but crushed that they hadn't acknowledged his grief too. So don't forget that men grieve too.

Sarah Damaska, North Branch, Michigan

The second thing I have to tell you about your desire to know what to say, before we dive into ideas about what to say, is this: even if you come up with the perfect thing to say (as if there is such a thing), it simply won't fix the hurt or solve the problem of the people who are grieving.

Does that take some pressure off? I hope so. Really, there is nothing you can say that will make their loss hurt less. It's going to hurt for a while. They're not looking to you to make sense of it or to say something they haven't thought of or something that makes it not hurt. Your purpose in saying something is to enter into the hurt with them and let them know they are not alone.

It's not up to you to say something that answers the significant questions they are asking. Those take some time to work through, and if they sense your willingness to linger with them a bit in the midst of the questions rather than offer simplistic answers, they're more likely to want to explore them with you down the road. It's not up to you to recommend the book they need to read, the counselor they need to see, the drug they need to take. You don't have to provide for them a recommended framework for thinking and feeling their way through their loss. Really, you just have to show up and say very little except maybe—and forgive me if this offends you, but I just don't know a better way to express it—"This sucks."

> An older lady from our church sat me and my brothers down and tried to prepare us for returning to school after the sudden death of our father. She said, "Death sucks!" I was shocked to hear that word come out of an adult woman and a Christian at that. But she said there is no other way to express what we were going through other than that it sucked! It was so helpful and funny to hear someone use a strong word to express the horrible situation we were in.
>
> Jordan, Washington

It's not up to you to make the pain go away, even though you would love to be able to do so. Grieving people are not expecting you to make the pain go away. They're really just hoping that you will be willing to hurt with them. That's what makes a great friend in the midst of grief! He or she comes alongside and is willing, at least for a while, to agree that this is terrible, unexplainable, the worst. No forced looking on the bright side. At least not yet. No suggesting you should be grateful for anything. At least not yet. To have a friend who, with a shake of the head and a sense of "How can this be?" refuses to rush too quickly past sharing a sense of agonized disappointment at the reality of death—what a gift.

A couple came who had lost a son. The wife looked at me at one point and said, "Someday this will be okay. Not today. Not tomorrow. But someday, it will be okay." I hung on to that. It had to be someone who had experienced this level of grief, though, in order for me to believe it.

Sharon Smith, Muncie, Indiana

So how do you begin to formulate what you might say when the time comes? It depends.

It depends on the nature of your relationship with the person. What we say to a business colleague will be different from what we say to a close, personal friend or family member.

It depends on where that person is in the process of grief. What we say on the day a loved one has died, or when we greet someone at the visitation, is likely different from what we might say a few weeks, a few months, or even a few years later.

Grieving people are as different from each other as—well, as different from each other as people are different from each other. What is helpful and meaningful to one person may be unwanted or even annoying to another. Words welcomed by one grieving person may be offensive to another. There are no one-size-fits-all words or deeds. There are just lots of hurting people who feel sad and lonely and are desperate to know that there are people around them who are willing to get outside of themselves to enter into their sorrow in a meaningful way.

Let's begin with the basics.

LET THE GRIEVING PERSON TAKE THE LEAD

Some people go through the visitation, funeral, or memorial service and the days immediately following with a great sense of strength, and they relish the interaction with people who have come around them at this difficult time. Others are worn out, overcome, and can barely converse with those who have come to express their sympathy.

Determine in advance and discipline yourself in the moment to listen more than you talk. Some of us have lots of words. We feel awkward with silence, so we tend to instinctually fill it up with words. But there is great power and comfort in simply showing up and being willing to sit in the silence and listen to the person who is grieving give voice to their regrets about the past, fears about the future, complaints about what others have said or done, rehearsals of the events that transpired, questions about God and life after death, chaotic thoughts, conflicting feelings, disappointments, desires, and despair. For good friends of the grieving, this companionship through grief is something that takes place over the long haul. It's not up to you to fix all of their faulty thinking every step along the way. Instead of driving the conversation, hold back. Take the humble position of letting the grieving person take the lead in when to talk and what to talk about.

Just because the words on the tip of your tongue are true doesn't make it okay to say them. Or perhaps *now* is not the time to say them. For example, yes, God is good. No question. But that doesn't mean it's appropriate or helpful for you to say to the person overwhelmed by the crushing news of a loved one's death, "God is good." Now, if the grieving person says to you, "I know that God is good," you can agree heartily, even mentioning some specific ways we know he is good that can be taken hold of in the midst of something that is not good at all! But even then, you will want to acknowledge that you are well aware that it still hurts. Let the grieving ones be the first to state their feelings or conclusions, and then follow their lead.

DON'T ASSUME

Sometimes grief is complicated by other emotions such as relief (especially if death occurred after an extended illness or intense suffering), anger (toward a doctor who made a mistake or the loved one who took his own life), or shame (whether justified or not). Some people have a deep sense of joy that their loved one is free of the pain or difficulty of this life. Others have a deep sense of dread that life will never be good again, and they simply can't stand the suggestion that it will.

We who have experienced a similar loss to the grieving person's have to be especially sensitive about making assumptions. I often find myself—out of a desire to connect and empathize— wanting to say, "I know you feel sad," and, "I know it hurts." But the truth is, I don't know. My experience of grief was mine, and theirs is theirs.

Sometimes we assume, for example, when people lose a parent, that they have lots of pleasant memories of that parent. Maybe they don't. Maybe they always felt belittled or unloved by that parent and have few, if any, good memories. Certainly that parent's death will bring about some significant feelings. Most of us, in the midst of grief, have mixed and even conflicting feelings. Don't assume you know what someone else is feeling.

We can tend to assume a lot of things that we probably shouldn't. Don't assume that those you are comforting are confident that the deceased is now in heaven. Don't assume they are relieved to be free of the heavy burden of care for someone who was sick a long time. Don't assume they want to feel better anytime soon. Don't assume they want to get married again.

Don't assume that because they are in the throes of loss, they have questions that aren't being answered or they feel abandoned by God. Maybe they have much more Scripture-saturated, Holy Spirit–given clarity than you do. Don't assume.

DON'T COMPARE

I'm not sure why, but we tend to compare pain: *This is harder than that. That would be worse than this.* You can't really compare pain. It all just hurts.

So when someone has lost a parent to natural causes, don't suggest that such a loss is so much easier than losing that parent to some other cause of death. When a couple loses an unborn child, don't say that it would be so much harder to lose a child who had lived with them.

> I wish people understood that this loss was uniquely mine. It could not compare with anything else. I did not want to hear about a loss of theirs or anyone they knew.
>
> Jeanne Pierce, San Antonio, Texas

Don't compare the grieving person's loss to your own loss or anyone else's. Let it be all about him or her and the loved one who has died.

DON'T FEEL THE NEED TO FIX

We hate loose ends. We want to end every conversation with everyone smiling and assured that everything will be just fine. But that's not always reality, and sometimes, what people need is to wrestle for a while with the ugliness and uncertainties rather than feel better and move on. Offering real comfort to those who are grieving is not about leaving them with a happy thought, but more about accepting where they are—whether that be happy or sad, confident or confused. We don't have to fix everything or make sense of everything in the course of our brief conversation. Instead, we can be willing to enter into the unanswered questions and unresolved conclusions and uncomfortable realities.

> When I expressed to a (well-meaning) friend how alone I felt, her response was, "But you are not alone! Every time you hear those words in your mind you need to fight! Go read Psalm 34; write it out! Keep it in your pocket! You are NOT alone." This, unfortunately, made me feel worse, like I had a spiritual problem on top of everything else.
>
> Doris, Ontario, Cananda

> Many friends were so eager for my pain to end that they encouraged me to have joy. They said that, because they did not want to see me hurt. But what they did not understand was that because of joy—the joy of the Lord—I could be sad.
>
> Donna, Texas

DON'T BE IN A HURRY

There might be lots of things you hope to talk about with a grieving person. But don't be in a hurry. Think of it as more like a marathon than a sprint. The day of the tragedy or the day of the visitation or funeral is not the time for talking through everything that will make sense of the loss and get that person on the road toward recovery. It is the time for simply coming alongside and being a companion in the sadness and questions. The day may come for a deep discussion. Or you may discover that you are not the one who the grieving person feels comfortable talking with about these things.

> I was often told that I was "doing so well." I started to feel like this was some goal I needed to attain, because it was something everyone seemed pleased to see in me. Yet, when the evenings came, I would find myself so stricken with tears and weeping that I physically couldn't move. I felt very alone that I was still so sad.
>
> Molly, Oregon

DON'T MAKE IT ABOUT YOU

To be honest I have a hard time believing some of the stories I've been told about people who, in the midst of the most difficult days of grief—at the visitation, the funeral, the burial, and in the early days after—added to the pain of those grieving by getting offended or complaining about not being included or consulted, by needing credit for all they were doing to help, or by seeking attention through their previous involvement with the deceased. And yet I also recognize that we all have warped ways of wanting to make pretty much everything about ourselves—including someone else's death or grief. We are sometimes so needy that we can resent the attention someone else is receiving in the midst of loss and subtly look for ways to get some of it for ourselves. Getting outside of ourselves isn't always easy. It requires that we focus on the hurting person rather than on our experience, our feelings, our desires, and our questions.

The truth is, if you have been through loss, sharing your

personal story with a grieving person may, at some point, help her not to feel alone. The way you have grown through grief and the good you have seen come from what you thought could only be bad may give her hope. But it is far better to be invited to share such stories. You may need to earn the right to be heard by being willing for now to keep her loss, not yours, as the centerpiece of your conversation. Your story of triumph that you think would give her hope may serve to make her feel that she must be doing this grief thing all wrong. The only story that needs to be told is hers—at least until you are invited to share yours.

In the helpful book *Don't Sing Songs to a Heavy Heart*, Dr. Kenneth Haugk says that if we are tempted to start a sentence any of the following ways, we may be shifting the focus to making it more about us than the person who is grieving:

"Well I . . ."
"When I . . ."
"I remember . . ."
"My . . ."[1]

But it just comes so naturally, doesn't it? It does to me. I love to talk about me. I find the subject of me infinitely interesting. But it is not always as helpful as I want to think it is. I have to learn and keep re-learning not to make it about me. Maybe you do too.

LISTEN MORE THAN YOU TALK

I know it's awkward. And many of us tend to want to fill up the awkward silence with many words. Yes, there will probably be an interaction requiring words in the receiving line. But if you hang around a little more, don't be afraid to simply be with the grieving person—sitting on a park bench or porch swing, going fishing, taking a drive, working in the garden, folding the laundry, baking some cookies—growing in your comfort with silence, giving the gift of quiet and unassuming companionship. Don't underestimate the power of your physical presence to bring comfort. Your presence—at the house, at the visitation, at the funeral, at the burial (if invited), and over the days, weeks, and months to come—is far more valuable than any words you can say.

> I need to talk about my mother, but sometimes, I cannot find the courage to begin the conversation.
>
> Donna, Maryland

Don't Tell Them What to Do

When we interact with those thrust into the unknowns of grief, and we want to help, we can sometimes assume a parental tone, telling them what they need to do or not do. Some people become instant preachers, experts, spiritualists, mothers, and advice dispensers in situations of grief. They tell the grieving person what he must remember, what he must do, what he must read, what he must avoid, what grief is going to be like, the counselor he needs to see, the medication he needs to take, the trip he needs to go on, the way he should think, act, and feel.

"You need to eat something."
"You need to go to bed."
"You ought to see a doctor."
"You don't want to do that."
"You've got to do this."

And here's the rub: you may be exactly right! But rather than talk down to him like a parent to a child, come alongside him to figure things out. Instead of giving an instruction as an authority, you might float a "I wonder if . . ." idea as a friend and see if it is taken hold of. Grieving people don't need us to tell them what to do. They are not looking for advice unless they ask for it. They do, however, need caring, wise, close-by friends to talk with them about decisions that need to be made in a time when it is hard to think straight.

> Someone said to me, "You never need to hide your true feelings from me; I won't judge you or tell you what to feel. You can just be who you need to be. I am safe."
>
> Vicki Font, Ontario, Canada

ESTEEM THEIR GRIEF

When we're grieving, we want to sense that the person we're talking to recognizes how significant our loss is, and what we really don't want is to sense that our loss is being minimized or dismissed as somehow *less than*. We minimize others' loss when we talk about what could be worse, implying that they should be grateful instead of sad, or when we seem to assume that because the deceased had lived a long life or had been sick for a long time or was not that close of a relation, the grieving one should not be quite so sad.

> Having been mostly raised by my grandmother, when she died, I felt a sense of grief similar to losing a mother. When I told people how I was feeling, occasionally there was judgment for the depth of feeling and loss. Some people would

compare my grief with their experience of losing grandparents and get confused about why I was taking it so badly and taking so much time to "get over it"!

Anonymous, Oxford, UK

Being the aunt (not the parent or grandparent) sometimes left me alone in my grief.

Connally Gilliam, Washington, DC

Even if you have experienced a very similar loss to that of the person you're talking to, make the choice to diminish your experience and esteem their loss.

Oftentimes when I talk to people who are going through grief, because they know that two of our children died, they say something like, "Well I don't have to tell you how this feels. You know." And, out of a desire to esteem their grief, I often say something like the following.

To a widow: "Well I have experienced loss, but I can't imagine how hard it must be to lose your partner and lover and best friend of forty years."

To a parent: "Well I have a sense of what this is like, but I don't know what it's like to lose a grown son in this way," or, "I do remember how much it hurt to lose Hope and Gabe, but today my heart hurts because of your loss."

To people in general: "Well, I've had a taste of what it's like to go through grief. But, of course, I don't presume to know exactly what your grief is like."

I appreciated anyone who did not minimize my pain. I was grateful for those who made me feel like my loss was great . . . because it was.

Allison Hucks, Nashville, Tennessee

DON'T BE PUT OFF BY TEARS

While tears can be awkward for everyone, tears are really such a gift. Tears have a way of washing away or carrying away the toxicity of the pain of grief. To shed tears is to release the tension and get the pain out in the open where it can be dealt with. When someone cries in your presence, don't be afraid that you made her cry. You don't have to apologize. You did not make her cry; you simply brought to the surface what was there anyway and needed to be released. Recognize that you have earned a trusted place, that she would be willing to share her tears with you.

> Look me in the eye and don't look away when I tear up. Holding my gaze may make you feel uncomfortable, but it allows me to share my pain.
>
> Mom, Minneapolis, Minnesota

Along with this, don't assume that what they really need is to be cheered up. It is a great gift to grieving people if those around them can be comfortable with their sadness, to not assume their sadness is a problem but rather that the deceased was of such value that their absence justifies great sorrow. A person who is sad doesn't necessarily need to be cheered up but needs time, space, and permission to simply be sad for a while.

When someone is crying or perhaps struggling to hold back tears, or feeling awkward about their tears, you can say:

"Your tears are beautiful. They reveal how deeply you love."
"You must have so many tears that want to come out. You can always cry with me."

"Of course it makes sense that you would cry. Your tears reflect how much [name of person who died] means to you." (Notice "means" and not "meant." The deceased's value is not a thing of the past.)

"Surely [name of person who died] is worthy of a great sorrow."

"Your tears are not a sign of weakness or a lack of faith. Your tears are a gift from God to help you wash away the pain."

"I feel honored you would be willing to share your pain with me by shedding tears."

"I wish I could carry for you some of the load of sadness you feel. I hope my tears tell you that while I can't take this away, I am right there with you."

"Cry as long as you need to."

Or you can say nothing and simply cry with them, making no effort to bring their tears to a halt. You can weep with those who weep (Rom. 12:15).

"Your tears are salve on our wound, your silence is salt."

Nicholas Wolterstorff[2]

DON'T ASK POTENTIALLY PAINFUL QUESTIONS OUT OF CURIOSITY

Lester and Bridgett were the first couple we knew close to our age who lost a child. Their daughter Emily died in the hospital after they took her to the emergency room for what seemed like a minor issue. I'll never forget Bridgett telling me about someone in our church who pressed for details on the autopsy. No mother wants to think about what happens to her child's body in the process of an autopsy, let alone talk about it.

People walked right up to me and asked how my brother took his life. I was stunned. How could they ask that? I had gone through the hellish nightmare of dealing with the coroner, etc. People's twisted interest in the details was way out of bounds.

Coley Fisher, Brea, California

Unless someone tells you that the deceased died by taking his or her own life, even when you may suspect it, don't ask. And if you are told, yet without details, don't ask. If he wanted to talk about it, he would. The same principle applies for deaths of all kinds. When someone dies, don't ask if the couple was living together. Don't ask if he was wearing a seat belt. Don't ask if she was a smoker. If the grieving person initiates a conversation about the spiritual condition of the deceased, then feel free to engage, sharing his sense of relief or his disappointment as the case may be. But don't ask.

Remember that when you're talking to those who witnessed the death or the dead body of someone they love, they have vivid mental pictures that come to mind when they talk about it. Their memories may include grimaces of pain, cries of agony, struggling for breath. Their mental pictures may be very bloody or very bleak and evoke feelings of regret and helplessness. Don't force them to relive those painful scenes in order to satisfy your curiosity.

But—and this is very important—be the kind of friend who is willing to listen when and if they do want to talk about those hard moments or the gruesome scene or the feelings of regret. Hopefully they will be able to do so at some point with somebody. If it is you, listen and let your heart be broken with theirs, and then keep the details to yourself. Such personal sharing is too sacred to be shared.

2

Typical Things People Say

(and What You Can

Say Instead)

In this chapter we're going to work our way through some of the things that are often said to grieving people from those who mean well but miss the mark, as well as what we might say instead. (And if you discover something here that you know you've said to someone a time or two, give yourself some grace. You're learning. I'm still learning. We're all still learning how to love others wisely and well.)

What People Say

We'll begin with some typical things that are said to those who are grieving, and then we'll consider how we might improve on them. Grieving people often hear:

Silly sentimental things such as, "I guess God just needed another angel in heaven."

Can't-you-just-look-on-the-bright-side things such as, "Well, at least you can have other children."

Sum-it-up-spiritually things such as, "It must have been God's plan."

Twisted-Scripture things such as, "You know that God will never give you more than you can handle."

Outright-wrong-but-spiritual-sounding things such as, "God needed her with him more than we needed her here."

Quazi-spiritual-but-ultimately-meaningless things such as, "I'm sending you good thoughts."

Put-on-the-pressure things such as, "Just think about how God is going to use you because of what you've been through."

I-have-the-answer-to-your-problem things such as, "Here is the doctor you need to go to, the book you need to read, the person you need to talk to."

We want to do better than this. With our words and with our manner and perhaps with our tears, we want to bring a sense of relief and safety to those who are hurting. That's take a closer look at those remarks.

"*I know just how you feel.*" No, you don't. You may have gone through grief before. You may have gone through a similar loss of a spouse or a child or a parent or a best friend. But you are not the one who has now lost his or her spouse, child, or parent. You are you, and that person is that person. Though you may be trying to offer companionship, this statement really just diminishes the other's loss because it seems to suggest that it is not really unique. Perhaps we say this because we think it will somehow help to give the grieving one a preview of what is ahead for good or for bad. But, really, that's just our pride talking—our desire to be an expert in this grief thing. Don't assume another's grief experience will be the same as yours. Your experience of grief makes you an expert on your grief, but not on someone else's.

Instead you might say, *when invited* to share about your own experience: "Just because I've experienced loss, I don't presume to know how this must feel to you, and I'm so sorry you have to bear it." Or you might simply ask, "What is your grief like these days?"

> We're so quick to say, "Oh, I know how you feel," and we usually add the word *exactly*: "I know *exactly* how you feel." I want to say, "No. Excuse me. You do not." The best we can do is to say, "My heart breaks for you. I have experienced grief, and my heart aches for you."
>
> Kay Warren[3]

"*You'll be fine.*" You mean to be encouraging. But what the grieving person hears you saying is that the person who died didn't really matter enough for his or her absence to matter. I remember a friend at church saying to me, "You'll be fine. You're strong." I probably just gave her a blank stare. But later I figured out what I wished I had said, which was, "I may be strong, but I'll never be fine." In that moment I felt like she just didn't get that this loss was changing everything about my life. It felt to me that she was diminishing my daughter, Hope, which hurt more than anything—like she was saying Hope's life ultimately wouldn't matter enough to knock me off my game.

When told I was strong, it felt like I wasn't allowed to show weakness. In being told to rely on God's strength and seek his peace, I wasn't allowed to express fear and disappointment. I know they meant well, but for me it meant I couldn't be real with them and couldn't process my grief, or reconcile my beliefs with my reality. It made it so hard.

Ruth, UK

Stop telling me to be strong. Let me be weak before Christ who strengthens me.

Casey Belgard, Denham Springs, Louisiana

Instead of saying, "You'll be fine," you might say: "I can't imagine how hard things are for you right now. I want you to know I'm going to be here with you in the hard times. And I'm going to believe with you—even when, and especially when it is hard to believe—that God is going to give you the grace you need to face every day, whatever it brings."

"*You can have more children.*" When you say something like this, the grieving person wants to scream in response, "Maybe I will, but I won't ever have this child with me again in this life, and that's what hurts! Another child will not replace this child." And when they do have another child, they really don't want you to suggest that this child has somehow "fixed" their grief or "filled" the place of the child who died. It just doesn't work that way. That child will certainly bring new joy, but that child won't have the ability to eliminate the lingering sorrow.

I just had a miscarriage this week. This was our first pregnancy and could be our last. We had trouble getting pregnant, and I'm thirty-eight, and we're not sure if we'll get another chance. A few people have said things like, "I know God will give you a child." We know they mean well, but those remarks are completely unhelpful, because we know they have no idea what God's plan is. It actually seems to put a wedge in between us and the people who say these things because I can't listen to someone who says what they think I want to hear, when it has no basis.

Brooke Holladay, South Carolina

Along the same lines is to say to the grieving widow or widower, "*You're young; you'll get married again.*" The widow or widower is missing the spouse who has died, and your suggesting that he or she can be easily replaced insults the person they love. And certainly don't ask the recently widowed if they are seeing anyone, because it subtly suggests this is the answer to their grief. If they are seeing someone and they want you to know, they'll bring it up.

Pretty much anything that starts with "*Well, at least . . . ,*" such as, "*Well, at least he didn't suffer*"; "*Well, at least we know where she is*"; or, "*Well, at least you still have your other children.*" When we say such things, we think we're helping grieving people to look on the bright side. We want to finish our conversation with them on a happy and hopeful note. But what they want are friends who are willing to sit with them in the darkness, feeling the weight of the loss with them. We think they need perspective. But what they need is time and freedom to lament their loss.

When one of those "Well, at least . . ." thoughts runs through your mind, let it stay there. You can think it. Just don't say it. And if the grieving person says something that begins with "At least . . . ," you can agree! As they "try on" a new perspective and seek after a heart of gratitude, you can affirm their conclu-sions. Just don't be the first one to say it.

> A pregnancy lost through miscarriage is nevertheless the loss of a baby. My hopes for that child, my dreams for my family, and my visions of the future died with that child. Saying things like, "It just wasn't meant to be," or "There must have been something wrong with the baby," or even, "You are probably better off," is terribly insensitive and damaging to someone who is already fragile. The only thing that helped was for people to acknowledge my loss as real, my grief as valid.
>
> Melissa, Gainesville, Florida

> If you think your task as comforter is to tell me that really, all things considered, it's not so bad, you do not sit with me in my grief but place yourself off in the distance away from me. Over there, you are of no help. What I need to hear from you is that you recognize how painful it is. I need to hear from you that you are with me in my desperation. To comfort me, you have to come close. Come sit beside me on my mourning bench.
>
> Nicholas Wolterstorff[4]

"*Well, at least now you can [fill in the blank].*" It's impor-tant to understand how conflicted grieving people, who have been "burdened" (our view but likely not theirs) by taking care of a loved one, feel that they now have time to do things they didn't have time for and the freedom to go places they couldn't go. To the grieving person, it feels wrong to have that freedom or to have their load lightened, and they don't want anyone to think they are celebrating or enjoying what was made possible by their loved one's death.

Instead of saying anything that starts with "Well, at least . . . ," you might say *nothing*. There's just not a good alternative other than silence when "Well, at least . . ." is what's going through your mind.

"Don't you think it's time to move on?" They have been so sad for so long. They seem so focused on their loss and unable to see or think or talk about anything else. You see their sadness and think the sadness is the problem. It isn't. They've lost someone they love, someone important and precious to them, and it makes sense that they would be sad for a while. Don't rush them. Don't tell them they need to move on. There is no timeline for grief, no appropriate or reasonable time frame for being really sad. But do encourage them to keep moving forward. Do you hear the difference? To hear "Move on" sounds and feels like leaving the person they love behind. And that prospect is awful. But the idea of moving forward toward healing and joy incorporates their very real grief and sadness with coming to acceptance and a new sense of normal.

Certainly some people get stuck in their grief. Grief, for some people, becomes a new identity; it comes to define them. Telling them to move on won't help but will likely cause them to dig their heels deeper into the mire of grief.

Instead of suggesting they move on, you might say: "I will never suggest that you 'move on.' I know the very idea of moving on hurts. It sounds like leaving behind the person you love. But I do so want you to discover some joy again. I want you to know that I will be here with you as you continue to move through this grief. And I look forward with you to the day when the sun seems to come out again in your life."

"This must be God's will." Where do we start with this?

Let's start with what people hear when we say this, which may be very different from what we intend to express. Grieving people hear:

God wanted your loved one to die.
God gave your mother the cancer that killed her.
God is happy that your loved one took his own life.
Even though this feels like a bad thing, it is really a good thing.
That drunk driver isn't responsible for the death of your loved one since really God did this.

I know what you're thinking. You're thinking that's not what you mean when you say such things, and surely the person you're talking to will understand what you mean and agree. When we're talking to grieving people, we have to be sensitive not only to what we say but to what they may likely hear in what we say. The problem with saying "It was God's will" to a grieving person is not with whether it's true. The problem is with how a grieving person likely receives this oversimplified statement in the midst of loss.

The truth is, the term "God's will" means many different things to different people. And it sounds very different in the days following the accident, the suicide, the unthinkable, than it did before, when it was merely a theological and not such a personal issue. I have come to think the term is our inadequate human language trying to make divine mystery manageable and tolerable. The words themselves are simply inadequate to carry the weight of the reality—especially when used in a simplistic way.

The plans and purposes of God and how he is bringing them about in his world are unfathomable to our limited human understanding. Since God is in control of the world he has made, we know that nothing happens in this world, or in our lives, that is outside of his control. How else could we have any confidence about anything God promises in the Bible about how he will bring human history into a glorious new beginning in the new heavens and the new earth, if he does not have the power to guide the course of history? If God is not ultimately in control of the world he has made, everything that happens in this world is random and meaningless.

Was it God's will for two of my children to be born with Zellweger syndrome and live very short lives? I don't think this question can be answered on these terms, nor does it need to be. We think we had two children who died because of the corrupting impact of sin on this world—the brokenness of this world has infiltrated even our genetic code so that we have defective genes. We don't think God picked us out to have two children who would die. But we would also say that nothing happens to us that is somehow outside of his control. God has ordained a world in which he accomplishes his will through secondary causes such as the laws of nature and human choice. As I've heard my friend Joni Eareckson Tada say, "Sometimes God allows what he hates to accomplish what he loves."

One of the ways we come to a sense of peace following the death of a loved one is by reckoning with the reality of God's providential guidance of all things and by coming to rest in the confidence that God is working out his plans for his creation and for his people in ways we cannot completely grasp from our limited purview. If you are invited into the grieving person's life to have a meaningful dialogue about this mystery, seeking together with Bibles open to come to a greater sense of God's sovereignty over his world, that is one thing. In fact it is a real privilege and responsibility. But resist the urge to insert "God's will" in a brief interaction.

I appreciate what Gregory Floyd writes in *A Grief Unveiled* about the loss of his son, Johnny, who was hit by a car in front of their home, on this issue of God's will:

> I am certain God received him with open arms, but I am not at all sure that he took him. "Taking him" by means of a car crash makes God the agent both of his death and of the undoubtedly great suffering of the man who hit him, to say nothing of all the other sufferings involved. The God of life does not go around setting up accidents. They happen because we live in a world broken by sin, a world of human freedom, and a creation that still groans in travail while awaiting its redemption. And yet, to be more honest than I want to be, I cannot attribute Johnny's death to "just an accident," as though God was nowhere near it. . . . The finite human mind cannot reach into the recesses of the infinitely transcendent mind of God. But the end of understanding does not mean the end of trust or love or obedience.
>
> I reached the point where I could only surrender to the mystery of God's will in the broadest sense of the word. At a certain point, a moment of grace, God's will ceases to be a problem and becomes a mystery. I must accept that God allows things to happen that he did not design, or accept that his designs, which initially transcend my capacity to understand, rest preeminent and secure and are never ultimately thwarted by evil.
>
> To see behind the loss and sorrow the hand of God is a severe grace.[5]

Instead of saying it was God's will or God's plan, you might say: "I don't presume to understand why God would include this in his plan for your life, and, honestly, it just doesn't make sense to me. Sometimes I just wish he would hurry up and put an end to death for good. But I'm asking God to give us the faith to trust his plans and his purposes and his timing."

> Theology is a grounding in ultimate hope, not a formula book to explain away each individual event.
>
> David Brooks[6]

"I would have liked to come to the funeral but . . ." All you need to say is that you are so sorry you were not there. Don't tell them why. It simply won't be a good enough reason from their perspective. It was the worst day of their lives, and they wanted the whole world to take notice.

> I felt like the world should have stopped. I could not understand why everyone should go on doing the things people do.
>
> Karen Oliveira, Contagem, Brazil

You might also consider asking if you could watch the video of the service with the person who is grieving, at some later time. This is something they would likely never ask someone to do with them but would be so grateful to share with someone who cares.

> Nine months after our son passed away we went on vacation with another couple, who had been unable to attend the

funeral. While on vacation we watched the video of our son that the funeral home had put together and listened to the funeral sermon. We cried together. We prayed together. It was an intensely spiritual time, and we felt bathed in the love and compassion of Jesus Christ.

Ellen Hekert, Mount Hope, Canada

Instead of saying *why* you weren't at the funeral or memorial service you might say: "I am so sad that I wasn't able to be there with you on the day you said good-bye. I really missed out by not being a part of that day and I would love for you to tell me what was especially meaningful at the service if you're up to sharing it with me."

"*You know that most couples that lose a child end up getting a divorce.*" Some couples that lose a child end up thinking they are destined to divorce because they hear such scary statistics from so many people. There's one problem: they're made up![7] Actually, a couple of scientific studies show the opposite is true. Now, it is true that grief puts a lot of pressure on a marriage. And couples have to really give each other a lot of grace as they navigate the road of grief. They are two individuals grieving in different ways and on different timetables, which can lead to lots of conflict as well as intense loneliness. But since this frightening and vague divorce statistic just isn't true, and isn't helpful, let's just put this myth to rest.

Instead of warning about the possibility of divorce you might say: "I am so sorry that the two of you have to experience this loss but so grateful you have each other. I'm praying that God will enable you to comfort each other well, even though you're both hurting so much."

"*The pain never goes away.*" People who have experienced

a similar loss often say this to someone who is grieving. Likely the intention is to communicate that they still feel a sense of loss. They want to assure the grieving person that the one who died will always be remembered and valued. But what grieving people often hear is, "You are always going to feel the same level of pain you feel right now. This is your new normal, so get used to it." That prospect is overwhelming. And that simply isn't true. More likely, there will be a place in them that is tender for a long time, a place, when pressed, that will feel the hurt. But as time goes on, the pain will likely not be as heavy and debilitating as it is at first.

I often say to people *who ask* what to expect in grief: "It's going to hurt a while. And the difficult truth is, it may get worse before it gets better. But you do not have to hurt this much forever. The pain you feel now does not have to become your new normal. Allow yourself to feel it, invite the Holy Spirit into the midst of it, dig deeper into the Bible than you ever have before because of it, and expect that God will do a work of healing in your life and emotions. You will never forget the one you loved. You will likely always miss him and wish he was here. And there will likely be a place inside you that remains tender. Tears may always come easily. But that does not mean that you forever have to feel the pain and weight of grief that you feel now. Your love for the person who died is not defined by the level of your ongoing misery."

After the loss of my mother I had many people say they were sorry and then comment, "It has been X years since my mom passed, and I still miss her." I found that reassuring and comforting. It told me I could take my time in healing.

Sandra Garman, Paso Robles, California

When we gather now there's always someone missing, his absence as present as our presence, his silence as loud as our speech. When we're all together, we're not all together.

Nicholas Wolterstorff[8]

Instead of saying that the pain never goes away, you might say: "I know that life will never be quite the same without him. But I am praying that God will give you joy in the midst of your sorrow. I'm praying that the day will come when, as you think of him, you will be able to smile and feel joy that he was here and not just sorrow that he is gone."

"Just call me if you need something." Grieving people are not going to call you if they need something. They need for you to figure out what they need and just show up and take care of it. Instead of waiting for them to call, call them when you're on the way to the grocery store to get their list so you can pick up and drop off what they need. Call them and tell them you're coming over on Thursday to mow their lawn, do their laundry, help them go through paperwork, etc. Call them and tell them that you'd like to pick them up to go to church, to the meeting, to the movies.

I will never forget the line of people at the cemetery. They passed by hugging my mother and all seven of my siblings as we put Daddy in the ground. All the words blur together, except that they would be there for us. I remember wondering what they meant. The following spring, after Daddy was buried, one neighbor drove up our mile drive and asked what he could do. Any fences need fixing? Any chores the boys need help with? He just came. Every time he came I remember thinking about that line of people at the graveside. They were loving people who meant well. This man did well. He just came. I don't remember if he ever actually had to do anything. But he came and offered his strength to help.

Anonymous

A friend of ours had recently lost his dad, so he was freshly acquainted with everything that has to be done to get through the funeral process. We were devastated, numb, helpless. He went with us to the funeral home and helped us answer the questions they asked. He walked with us into that dreadful showroom of caskets and helped us select a moderately priced vessel for our priceless son. He helped us word the obituary. Then he gave his business card to the funeral director and said, "Send the bill to this address." We were stunned, almost too heartbroken to acknowledge the gift. But we will never forget it.

John Dobbs, Monroe, Louisiana

Instead of telling them to call if they need anything, you might say:

"Do you need to have any suits or dresses cleaned for the funeral? I will take them and get them back to you."

"I'm planning to mow your lawn the rest of the summer, so there's one less thing you have to think about."

"Can we keep your pets while you travel to the funeral?"

"I'm really pretty good with doing taxes. Could I come over and help you get your tax information together?"

"I'd really like to help you whenever you feel ready to go through his things. I'm not rushing you, but I would like to help when you're ready."

"I'd like to go out to the grave sometime soon. Do you want to go together?"

"Do you want to ride with me to the program at school?"

"We knew going out to buy a Christmas tree this year might be hard, so we've brought one over. Would you like for us to set it up for you?"

"We know your anniversary would have been this weekend. Could we come and take you out to lunch? We'd love to hear you tell about how the two of you met and fell in love."

If you ask me what I need, and I say nothing or I don't know, that is probably truthful and full of lies at the exact same time—not because I want to lie to you, but I honestly have a hard time processing that question.

Todd Storch, Coppell, Texas

"*I guess God just needed him/her in heaven more than we needed him/her here.*" This is one of those ridiculously sentimental, quasi-spiritual things that dishonors God and trivializes the grieving person's sense of loss and pursuit of answers to spiritual questions. Instead of saying that God must have needed the person who died or some other silly thing, you might say: "It is so hard to think about life here without [name of person who died.] I miss her already."

"*I know someone else who . . .*" When we hear about someone's loss, our brains begin a search like a computer, looking for a connection. And because we don't know what else to say, and in an effort to fill the awkward silence, we tend to blurt out the first "search result" that comes up: "I knew a family who had this happen . . . I knew a widow who . . . I heard about a person who . . ."

We want to demonstrate that we are familiar with the situation and aware of the implications because we know about someone else who experienced something similar. Somehow it makes us feel better to demonstrate our knowledge or connection, but it doesn't make the grieving person feel better. I promise you, it doesn't. To the grieving person, it feels like a subtle effort to diminish their loss.

The story of someone else's loss and triumphant response can come across like an example that the grieving are expected to live up to. And they don't appreciate the pressure. Or sometimes it can seem as if they are supposed to find some space in their hearts to feel sad for those other people you're telling them about. But they just can't. At least not right now. All of their capacity for sorrow is being used on themselves.

Instead of telling a story about someone else, you might say: "Some people seem to want to compare loss. But it all just hurts to the person who has experienced it. I'm so sorry you are hurting."

"*God took him so that . . .*" It is one thing to identify something good that has come about as a result of someone's death. It is quite another to suggest that good thing is the *reason* the person died. We simply can't trace or reduce or interpret the ways of God this simply. God is at work in the world doing many things, bringing about his plans and purposes. And while we might witness God use the death of someone in particular ways, that doesn't mean that's *why* he died.

Instead of presuming upon God's purposes, you might say: "I know that we'll never understand exactly why this has happened, but I am praying that God will pull back the curtain to allow you to see ways in which he is using it for good."

I know, I know, enough of these wrong things to say. But I

have to give you one more, because just a few days ago I said it myself. I said the most typical thing people say to grieving people. And the minute I said it, I wished I hadn't. I should know better. Here's what I said, or more accurately, what I asked: "How are you?"

It doesn't seem so wrong, does it? It's a question that reveals that we care. It lets the person know we haven't forgotten about their loss. Really, it is an invitation for the grieving to talk about their loss. But many grieving people say they simply hate the question. They feel put on the spot to report on their job performance in this task they've been given—continuing to live when their loved one has died—a task for which they had no training and for which they seem to have no resources. It's a question they don't know how to answer. "I'm fine" isn't quite right. They may be functioning and perhaps even feeling better, but they know they're not fine. "I'm terrible" seems whiney. "I'm angry!" seems unacceptable. "I'm crying all the time" seems pathetic.

"How are you?" is one of those questions that always bothered my husband, David, in those days after our daughter, and later our son, died. He always felt that he was supposed to quantify his progress back toward normalcy. In our book, *When Your Family's Lost a Loved One*, he wrote, "In the midst of my own pain and confusion, I suddenly also felt responsible to others to give an account for my progress. As the words of my reply came measured through my lips, I wondered if my report would be acceptable."[9]

The grieving person knows what the questioner most likely wants to hear—that everything is getting better, the world is getting brighter, the darkness is lifting, and the tears are subsiding.

But oftentimes that just isn't the way it is, and it can be awkward to be honest about the confusion, listlessness, and loneliness of grief. The reality of grief is that sometimes right after the loss we feel strong, but as time passes and the dailyness of life without the loved one settles in, we feel weak and weepy. And it can be awkward to talk about.

We're afraid that if we tell you how sad we are, you might think there is something wrong with the way we're doing this grief thing. Perhaps you think we should be on a steady upward path toward normalcy and that we're going in the wrong direction. Sometimes we want to scream that we will never be normal again. And sometimes we just want to say, "How am I? I'm sad. And I wish the world—including you—would simply give me some time and space to simply be sad. This person I loved has died, and I miss him. He mattered to me, and therefore it makes sense that I would not get over his absence easily or quickly."

There was a man in our church who had lost his wife, and during our time of trauma, any time we would see him, he would never ask, "How are you?" but rather would say, "Sharon, how good to see you!" usually accompanied by a hug. This allowed a relationship and conversation other than answering the dreaded question. He just knew. He was safe.

Sharon Smith, Muncie, Indiana

Following the deaths of my twin boys, a friend wanted to check in on me daily to know how I was doing. However, I was so overwhelmed by my grief that I often had trouble verbalizing my feelings. She began to simply ask me to rate how I was doing each day on a scale of 1 to 10. If my number that day was really low, she would press in, ask questions, and listen. On days that my number was higher, she would help draw my attention to those things that brought joy or relief in the midst of the pain. This simple technique was invaluable in that it met me where I was in my brokenness, it allowed me to say as much or as little as I was able, and it gave me the freedom to be real in my grief.

Angela Taylor, Dallas, Texas

Instead of asking, "How are you?" you might ask:

"What is your grief like these days?" This question assumes that it makes sense that the person is sad and gives them the opportunity to talk about it.

"I can't imagine how hard it must be to face these days without [name of person who died]. Are there particular times of day or days of the week you're finding especially hard?" Keep on saying the name of the person who died. It is music to the grieving person's ears.

"I find myself really missing [name of person who died] when I [fill in the blank]." It is a great comfort for the grieving person to know that he or she is not the only one who misses the person who died.

"I often think of you when I'm [gardening/driving by your house/going for a walk/getting up in the morning/etc.] and whisper a prayer for you to experience God's comfort. Are there particular things I could be praying for you as you go through this time of grief?"

"I know that [deceased's] birthday/deathday is coming up and it must be so very hard to anticipate that day without her here. What are you thinking about that day? Is there anything we could do to help you get through that day?"

"I know [the holidays/Mother's Day/Father's Day/your anniversary] is coming up. I will be especially thinking of you and praying for you as that approaches. We would love to have you over. Would you join us?"

In a sense, all of these questions are asking, "How are you?" but somehow they express a desire to enter into the sorrow of another instead of merely getting a report on their sorrow.

> We are learning so much in our grief. We are eager to share and process these things with others. It's so helpful when we don't have to be the ones to bring it up. When the opportunity presents itself, it is so helpful when you ask good, open-ended questions. We want to talk, and share, and recount, and remember, and give testimony of God's faithful work in the midst of our sorrow and pain. It's such a blessing when you provide us the opportunity to do this.
>
> Eric and Jodi Blick, Omaha, Nebraska

SO WHAT ELSE *CAN* YOU SAY TO SOMEONE WHO IS GRIEVING?

Believe it or not, one of the best things you can say is, "I don't know what to say." I know, it sounds weak. But that's the beauty of it. It reflects humility. It communicates that you don't presume to have words that would make the loss okay. It esteems their loss as being too great to minimize by mere sentiment. You can always say:

"I'm so sorry for your loss."
"I'm so sad with you."
"I really miss [name of the deceased]."

"You can be sure that [name of the deceased] will not be forgotten. I will never forget him."

"One of my favorite memories of [name of the deceased] is . . ."

"I thought of [name of the deceased] the other day when . . ."

"I don't presume to have anything to say that would make this okay. But I do want you to know how much I care."

"I wish I could take some of the pain you're feeling and bear it for you. I know I can't, but I want you to know I am feeling it with you."

"I don't know why this has happened."

"I'm so sorry you have to go through this."

And sometimes you don't have to use words at all.

I have had three miscarriages with little to no acknowledgment of the loss of these lives. However, an elder in our church came up to me, hugged me, kissed my forehead, and walked away. I cried all day because of that connection. I still cry when I think about it. The message I received was: I know, I am sad for you and it's okay where you are at in your grief, and you are loved.

Melissa Edwards, Los Angeles, California

On the day that our eighteen-year-old son died, my phone was ringing ceaselessly. One friend in particular was sitting next to me. In all of the noisy talk and movement around, he just sat there, and every once in a while he rubbed his hand across my shoulder and squeezed. He didn't say a word. Finally after a while of watching me answer my cell phone over and over he said, "Would you like me to take that and answer your calls for you?" He took the phone, and I didn't have to answer any more questions. Six and a half years later I remember that moment with such clarity and realize what a true friend can contribute in a moment of intense grief: silent presence.

John Dobbs, Monroe, Louisiana

In my survey of people who lost someone they loved, I noted two things in particular that grieving people told me over and over again that they really *want* people to say to them.

First, *grieving people long to hear stories about the person who died and specific things she said or did that were meaningful and memorable.*

It doesn't require a seminary education or a counseling degree. It just requires a little effort in scouring your memory bank: grieving people long to hear stories about the person who died and specific things she said or did that were meaningful and memorable. They're looking for something specific rather than general. They want something beyond "He was a really good guy," or, "She really made me laugh." They want to hear or read about a specific experience you had with the person who died that demonstrated he was a "good guy." They want to hear something specific he said that made you laugh. Instead of hearing that he was "always there for you," they want to hear about a specific time and way the one who died helped you.

If you can write down your memories of the deceased so that the grieving person can read them now and also save them for later, your thoughtfulness becomes a gift that keeps on giving. And if the grieving one is active on social media, to post your memory online and invite others to share similar stories is a great way to get other friends in on this joyful remembering.

> The responses that I treasure most of all are stories about Allison that I hadn't heard before, stories that painted her personality more clearly, maybe in ways that were new to me; stories that illustrated her beauty. There weren't very many of those. Many people said, "Allison was such a special person. She was so loving," which was good to hear but wasn't enough. There were a few people, though, who could say things like, "Do you know, Allison was in my Sunday school class and every week she . . ."
>
> Luke Veldt[10]

> I found it extremely meaningful when people took the time to write down memories of my parents in a card, letter, or email. It was encouraging to know that they had touched the lives of others and were being remembered—everyday memories and life events that had been shared together and were obviously being cherished by others. There were so many beautiful words written that made us feel we weren't alone on this journey. I have kept them all so I can go back and read them at a later date.
>
> Abi Byrd, Round Hill, Virginia

> The first Christmas after my husband died, his family had a ring of pillar candles, and each sibling lit a candle and told a funny story about Carl. I was able to hear some stories that I had never heard before.
>
> Linda Rhoney, Greer, South Carolina

> Even two years later, I want to hear stories about my husband, Patrick. I want to hear how you had a thought or memory about

him. Even if it brings up tears, I want to hear the stories and know he's not forgotten and that his godly legacy continues.

Dena McGoldrick, Clinton Township, Michigan

When I lost my dad to Alzheimer's, it was so meaningful to hear exactly how he had touched the lives of others. Many people told me specific ways he had helped them spiritually and practically that I had not known about before he died. He was a man known for his humor, so I also enjoyed hearing about the joy he brought to others. Even the short stories or sentiments shared on Facebook or by email were meaningful to my mom, my sister, and me.

Darla Knoth, Springfield, Missouri

I found it helpful when people were able to tell me stories about my sister—about their experiences with her that I wasn't there for, about her caring for them in such beautiful ways, about the meaning her life had while she was here, and how she will be missed. It helped me to know I was not alone in my grief.

Nancy Clausen, Chicago, Illinois

Don't bring me flowers. I can't bear to watch anything else die. And don't bring me a plant either. I have enough to take care of during my grief that I can't even take on the responsibility of watering a plant. I spend all day being sad, and I forget to water it. So I end up watching it die. I've watched enough death. Bring me your memories of my loved one; those I can hold onto forever!

Deanna McClain, Glenside, Pennsylvania

I treasure the stories that his friends told me that gave me a window into who our son was when he was away during those

college years. Also, friends wrote us letters of their memories
of our son as a child and teenager.

Renee Draughon, Nashville, Tennessee

I never forget my husband or our memories, but it's a comfort
to know others haven't forgotten either. My daughters especially love to hear memories and stories about their daddy!

Kristi Katches, Vista, California

One of my son's classmates wrote on a full notebook page
all the things she remembered about him from kindergarten
through school. I have reread it many times, and it will be
saved for his boys to read.

Jan Kelley, Wichita, Kansas

I was ten when my mom died in a car accident. What was
most comforting was when people would tell me positive
things about my mom that I didn't know: things she had done
to bless them, or ways she had lit up their world. She had really struggled with depression, and it was reassuring to know
that other people saw the good in her besides me.

Jacki Balfour, Manitoba, Canada

Wondering what else you might say that is meaningful? Here's
what some people who have been there say was meaningful to
them:

I wish people would say, "Tell me about your mother. What was
she like?" and not be afraid to sit and listen to my stories. I am
an introvert, so I tend not to tell stories unless people ask.

Sandra Garman, Paso Robles, California

One of the most helpful things that several of my friends said
to me repeatedly was, "I miss her too," or "I wish she was here

with us today." Letting me know that they too felt the sting of her loss helped me not feel quite so alone in my grief.

Lacy Smith, Rolling Meadows, Illinois

What means the most to me is friends who marked their calendar with his birthday and deathday and always sends a note to say, "I remember." Blessed gift!

Lisa Hellier, Macon, Georgia

Joshua lived for about thirty minutes outside the womb. Lots of folks said they were looking forward to meeting Joshua in heaven. That was helpful in that it confirmed the reality that we believe that that is where he is and that we will see him again.

Heather Etner, Vienna, Virginia

A friend wrote me a note after the passing of our son. In it she said, "Life will never be the same for you. And I just want you to know, no matter what your life is going to be like, I will always be in it with you."

GriefShare facilitator, Tampa Bay, Florida

The best thing anyone has ever said to me after the death of my daughter was, "I do not understand what you are going through or why this happened but I am here for you and grieve with you."

Mary Ellen Ashworth, Fayetteville, Georgia

When my husband and I lost our first child (stillborn at thirty-eight weeks) I had one friend send me a congratulations baby card. I loved the fact that she recognized that I was a mom and that we had a beautiful baby! It was my ray of sunshine in my stormy days that I'll never forget!

Courtney Carpenter, Seneca, Kansas

One of the pastors told me that my three-year-old child fulfilled his ministry in the time he lived with us. It was comforting to know that my son did what he was sent to accomplish.

Christine Johnson, Anderson, California

My friend Kathi Lewis wrote to me after my mother died: "She was the person who knew you the longest and loved you the most. Losing a mother is so hard. May the memories of your childhood and beyond sustain you. My prayers are with you."

Cherylee Deitrich, Wilmington, Delaware

I appreciated reading in a card, "No one has the words that will remove your sorrow, but we hope you find comfort in knowing there are many who wish they could."

Rosi Braatz, Lakeville, Minnesota

A dear friend, who has been through her own deep loss, said to me, "I don't have anything to tell you that will make the pain go away, but I know it helps to have someone listen to you talk about your loved one without making you feel like they're uncomfortable or they can't wait till you're finished. So I just want you to know that anytime you want to talk about Mark, I'm here to listen as long as you need me to. It doesn't even need to make sense."

Rosanne Haaland, Johnson City, Tennessee

I received a note from someone who does not know me well— really, an acquaintance—who said that she sees my dad's contagious smile in my smile. Being compared to my dad in such a kind way meant the world to me.

Catha Jaynes, Houston, Texas

I had my second child soon after my mother's passing, and it was very sweet, encouraging, and heartwarming that others would say how much my mom would have loved a specific time with or characteristic of my new baby.

Blair Therit, Raleigh, North Carolina

THINGS TO ASK OR SAY ABOUT THE DECEASED

I'm here to listen as long as you need me to.

What was she like?

I miss her too.

I remember . . .

I will always be in it with you.

I am here for you.

Losing a mother is so hard.

No one has the words that will remove your sorrow.

I see your dad's contagious smile in your smile.

Finally, the second thing people told me they really want people to say to them—and this may be the most powerful way you can bring comfort to someone who is grieving—is to *keep saying the name of the person who died.*

Oh, to hear that person's name. It is like salve to an aching soul, music to a heart that has lost its song. So many people get uncomfortable with speaking of the deceased by name. So when someone keeps speaking of him or her with joyful remembrance, it does something nothing else can do. It doesn't have to be a big deal or an emotional conversation. The more natural, the better. You can say things like:

- "I thought of Bob the other day when we were getting barbeque. I always loved how he made such good barbeque. I wish he had taught me his secrets."

- "Every time I pass a biker on the road, I think of Cheryl and how she always amazed me with her stories of the rides she went on. It makes me miss her."

- "I was thinking about Barb the other day and wondering what life is like for her now in heaven. I bet she is enjoying the beauty there. She always had such an eye for beauty."

- "Remember those big curls David had? I was always kinda jealous of his hair."

- "I wish Todd were here at the game with us. What do you think he'd have to say about those refs?"

- "When all the children got up to sing in church this morning, I couldn't help but notice that someone was missing. It hurt that Allison isn't here."

You never remind me of it; it's always on my mind, and I think about my son all the time. I may be "getting on with my life," working, being busy with things, but I love when anyone brings up his name and says anything about him.

Rachel Andrea, Cape Breton, Canada

One couple set a place at their wedding table for my son with a place card in his name and put his favorite soda there and took a picture to send me.

Jeanne Pierce, San Antonio, Texas

When my friends introduce me, they still say, "Kara has five children: four here and Selah, who is in heaven," or something along those lines. It means so much that they still remember her as part of our lives.

Kara Chupp, Portland, Oregon

I say and hear each of my kids' names dozens of times a day,
except for Annie. And that makes me so sad. When someone
talks to me and uses her name, it is deeply meaningful.

Sarah Damaska, North Branch, Michigan

As we come to the end of this chapter with all of its do's
and don'ts about what to say and what not to say, perhaps
you are realizing that you have really blown it with someone,
maybe with many people. It is never too late to ask forgiveness
for what you said or didn't say in the midst of someone's grief.
Yes, it will be humbling. Maybe it will be awkward. But most
likely you will find forgiveness. And more than that, the barrier
between you and that person will disappear and a fresh and
deeper friendship will take root.

3

Assumptions We Make That Keep Us Away (and Why We Should Simply Show Up)

Some of you are really ready to move on from what to say, because words aren't really your thing. You want to get busy. You want to *do something* tangible, helpful, and meaningful for the grieving person. You just need a good idea or to be pointed in the right direction. Well, then, the next two chapters are for you. Let's dive in.

If I had to boil down the message of this entire book to just two words, these two would probably cover it: *show up*.

Or, to put it another way, don't disappear; don't avoid. Enter in. Engage. I can't remember much of what anyone said to me in those early, hard days of grief, but in my mind's eye I can see the faces of all the people who showed up! They were there at the hospital when we handed over Hope's and Gabe's bodies.

They were there at the grave when we put their bodies in the ground. They were there at our house doing little projects, or not just bringing a meal but sticking around to share it with us. They sent a check to the memorial fund. They left flowers at the grave. This many years later, they still let me know when they put on their Christmas tree the ornament that has Hope's picture on it. All of these are incredible ways people have made a point to show up in our experience.

Yet even as I remember how people did it for us, and as I tell you to do it, I realize how many times I simply haven't done it for others. I have let selfishness or awkwardness or busyness or just apathy keep me from showing up too many times. Maybe you have too.

Showing up sounds simple. So why don't we do it? I think there are several reasons (besides that lame excuse of being too busy). We have offered to help but they haven't called, so we stay home. We figure they have other, closer friends who are taking care of them and that they probably wouldn't want us around since we don't know them well. We think they probably just want their privacy, to be left alone. We're simply afraid of saying or doing the wrong thing. So let's just deal one by one with each of these reasons for staying away.

"I told them to call if they need anything. What else can I do?" As I said earlier, they're not going to call if they need something. They don't have the clarity or the energy for it. Nobody wants to call and ask someone to come over and wash their dirty clothes or mow their lawn or clean their toilets even though that's what they really need. Nobody enjoys being needy. To ask someone to help with filing the insurance claims, picking out a gravestone, addressing thank-you notes, or pack-

ing away your loved one's things seems like a big ask, so the grieving person probably won't. What they really need is for you to figure out what they need and either ask if you can do it with them or for them, or just show up and take care of it.

> I wish people had understood that when they said things like, "We are here for you, whatever you need, just ask," it wasn't helpful. Often they were hurt when I didn't ask, and then I needed to manage those tensions in our relationship in addition to everything else we were dealing with. Many days I didn't know what I needed help with. I just felt alone and like I was drowning. Offering help but not taking initiative practically pushes the responsibility onto the person who is grieving and adds yet another burden.
>
> Abi Byrd, Rolling Hill, Virginia

I hardly know where to start when I think about the people in our world who simply showed up and did what we wouldn't have asked them to do but nevertheless needed to be done. And when I think about them, I have to fight back tears. There's something so deeply touching about remembering the people who showed up.

Our small group showed up from the very start, putting up our Christmas tree and decorating it. John came over and hung the lights outside with David. Mary Bess set up and oversaw a calendar of people who brought meals. Mary Grace was the contact for people who just wanted to come over and be with us. Jan took us out for a day on their boat, and we called the day, "Hope Floats." Lynn recruited and directed all of the best musicians in Nashville to make the music at Hope's memorial service, and later Gabe's, beyond glorious. Marty came over and helped me do the hard thing of putting away some of Hope's things to make it ready for being a guest room again. Joanna came over after and got rid of all the dying flowers in the house that were such a vivid reminder to me of what was happening to Hope's body in the grave. Dan and Sue planted a tree in their yard in Hope's memory and brought me cuttings of the blossoms. Bonita came over and helped me get all of Gabe's stuff organized for his short little life spent in our bedroom. Ed brought back the crib we had given away after Hope died, thinking we wouldn't need it again, and then came and got it again after Gabe died. Just the other day, sixteen years down the road, Mary went with me out to the cemetery to talk with them about repairing Hope and Gabe's gravestone that has deteriorated.

And, really, that doesn't begin to tell all the ways people showed up in our experience. But maybe that begins to give you some ideas for how you can show up for others. Or maybe you'll get some ideas from the people who shared with me how their friends showed up in incredible ways:

> One of my best friends came to my house and helped me pack for the funeral, which was out of town. Another friend watched our dog while we were away, and yet another friend stocked our freezer with meals and picked us up at the airport. None of them asked, "What can we do?" or, "Please call if you need anything." They just saw a need and filled it. I will never forget these very practical kindnesses.
>
> Jeanne Pierce, San Antonio, Texas

> When our son was killed in an auto accident just three days before he was to leave for college, one of our dear friends

came over and asked for a list of who she could call for us. Our son still had braces, so my friend called the orthodontist and canceled his appointment. She called the college to inform them. She also took our laundry home and the dress our daughter would wear for the funeral and washed and pressed everything.

Phyllis Dengler, Sterling Heights, Michigan

One of Dave's fellow school board members owned a car wash. He washed and vacuumed my family's cars to use in the funeral procession.

Susan, Nebraska

My friends Diana and Rosemary came in and cleaned the house, changed bed linens, and organized food for us. Diana came every day until I made her leave. I will never forget walking into my kitchen and seeing her on her hands and knees scrubbing my kitchen floor, knowing she is not much of a housekeeper at her own home. She knew there were no words she could say, but her actions spoke loudly!

Jimmy Lou Allred, Foley, Alabama

Ella died the day after Thanksgiving. On Christmas morning my daughter and son-in-law's friends assembled on their front lawn. There must have been fourteen of them, and most had to arrange for sitters on Christmas Day! They sang them songs, sweet ones, funny ones, ones with props, and just loved them. It had to have been one of the sweetest outpourings of love I have ever seen.

Debra Toombs, Long Beach, California

We had put up our Christmas tree and before we could decorate were called to be with my dad. Following the funeral and our time with my mom, we returned home. When we entered our house, we discovered that our Christmas tree had been decorated by the ladies from my Bible study class with the most beautiful, homemade paper snowflakes that contained handwritten Bible verses, reminders of God's promises, and prayers for our family. It was the most stunningly gorgeous tree ever and a time our family will always remember. We saved the snowflakes and add some to our tree each Christmas!

Pam, Pennsylvania

My parents died ten weeks apart, and I made five long-distance trips that summer to care for them, plan funerals, and attend to the legal and financial matters that followed. When I finally got home, I was busy catching up at work. It meant so much that two of my friends took it upon themselves to mow and rake my lawn—not just for a week or two but for the rest of the season!

Beth, Minnesota

We had friends text us from the grocery store: "I am picking up some coffee, milk, bread, and cereal for you. What else do you need?" It was such a blessing when friends would offer to take our kids out for a bit: "We are headed to the pool and would love to take your kids with us." "We have an extra ticket for the ball game; would your daughter like to come with us?" "Would your kids like to go get some ice cream this evening?" It gave the kids a break from the sadness and tears and gave us the opportunity to freely process some of the more raw grief alone as a couple.

Jodi Blick, Omaha, Nebraska

I had a friend who dropped her kids off with a babysitter every Tuesday morning and came over to my house just to be there to help me in any way I needed. She helped me cook, paint the trim around my house, and many other things. But most importantly, she was there to love and care for me. She did this for months and months after our daughter passed.

Ashley Sinclair, Greenville, South Carolina

I had a friend who came over with plants to plant in my yard. Digging with her and having new plants to water was a helpful project and sweet time with her. I knew she was caring for me.

Kim, Kansas

My best friend took me to a daytime baseball game. It was such a beautiful, sunny day, and it felt good to be outside and among the crowd, and baseball is kinda slow so you can actually have good conversations during the game.

Kellly Hughes, Chicago, Illinois

What beautiful ways of showing up!

Maybe before we move on, we should, however, offer a little caveat to the "show up and do what needs to be done" maxim. It isn't helpful when someone does something that the grieving person doesn't want done or when someone forces help when it isn't needed or wanted. I remember the day after our son Gabe died, someone, seeking to be helpful, washed all of his clothing and bedding. And I was so disappointed when I discovered it. I wanted to hold on to some of the unwashed items he had worn. I wanted to cover myself in a blanket that had covered him and smell his smell.

Also, it is not helpful to be so anxious and insistent on helping that we actually become a burden on the grieving person. And it's just kind of annoying when people seem to be inserting themselves in such a way that it appears that they are more interested in getting credit for what they've done than simply being of help. (Though I must admit I loved it when our friend Sue showed up at our house and gave us a laugh by saying, "Tell me what I can do that will require the least effort but get the most glory.")

THINGS YOU CAN DO FOR THE GRIEVING

Help pack	*Wash and vacuum the car*
Watch the dog	*Clean the house*
Stock the freezer	*Mow or rake the lawn*
Offer to make calls	*Take out the kids*
Wash and press clothes for the funeral	*Bring groceries*
	Plant plants

Another reason we don't show up for grieving people is that we think, *I don't know them well. They probably only want to be with close friends.* We assume they don't want to be bothered. We assume that someone else who knows them better is taking care of them. But that isn't necessarily true. Certainly it means a great deal when long-term and even long-lost friends come around us. But the season of grief is also a time when new friendships are forged.

My husband, David, and I hold weekend retreats, called Respite Retreat, for couples who have faced the death of a child.[11] At these events I often ask for a show of hands from those who feel that they had good, close friends who, for some reason, seemed to disappear in the midst of their grief—friends who didn't seem to get it and couldn't seem to enter in. And usually pretty much every hand goes up. And then I ask them to raise their hand if there were people—people they were not particularly close to or perhaps didn't even know before their loss—who showed up in incredibly meaningful ways. And usually every hand goes up again. A sense of joyful appreciation comes over them. Some of the frustration over friends who disappeared gives way to gratitude for the new friends who came into their lives in the midst of loss.

When I think back to our experience of grief, I see faces of people—people we didn't really know before then who were brave enough to enter in. The truth is, some of the people who were closest to us, people we thought would be there with us, simply didn't know how to share it with us in a way that was meaningful. And in some cases our friendship was just never the same again. But at the same time, there were people who weren't close to us who showed up. Many of them became treasured friends while others went back out of our lives. But there is such a special bond that remains, a sweetness when we see them, because they showed up at the lowest point of our lives.

> A woman I had never met brought us dinner when she heard at church about our grief. And while she stood in my kitchen, she cried. No one else from church who knew us had grieved so well with me.
>
> Lindsey Coffman, Milford, Kansas

> A dear woman in my church told me that the Lord had laid it on her heart to pray and fast for me as I grieved my twin sons who died as a result of being born prematurely. Though she did not know me well, she would periodically tell me how he was consistently bringing me to mind and how she was faithfully praying for our family during the darkest days of our grief.
>
> Angela Taylor, Dallas, Texas

A third thing we assume about people going through grief is, "*they probably just want to be left alone, and I don't want to intrude.*"

It's true that many grieving people simply don't want to deal with others. They don't want to have awkward conversations and uncontrolled emotions. They want to be alone—to have time to think and reflect and simply miss the person who is gone.

But here's what grieving people wish others would understand: grief is incredibly, relentlessly lonely. It really makes a huge difference to be reminded that we are not forgotten, that our loss is on the radar of people around us. We are really hoping that someone will be interested in just being with us rather than being interested in "fixing" us. We're hoping that someone will refuse to be intimidated by the awkwardness and will simply enter into the mess—someone who is not bothered by the bathroom that hasn't been cleaned and the clothes that haven't been put away and the hair that hasn't been combed.

> I used to assume that I shouldn't bother people, but now whenever a friend suffers a loss, I pick up the phone and call right away.
>
> Debra Toombs, Long Beach, California

We feed daily on the kindness of others even though the interactions are sometimes awkward. No, we probably don't want you to drop by unannounced at inconvenient times. No, we probably don't want you to bring your five kids when they're cranky and need a nap. But we don't want you to stay away. We don't want you to assume that we want to be alone. We don't want you to assume that because we don't know you well, you are not welcome. We really need for you to be persistent in offering us companionship. We need you to persevere in inviting us back into the land of the living. So don't give up too easily on us.

> In my early grief I withdrew and isolated myself. Most people gave up on me pretty quickly, but one neighbor called me every week, leaving messages telling me she was praying for me and thinking of me and wanted to go to lunch whenever I felt up to it. She was concerned and never gave up on me. We still meet for lunch often, and she has become a good friend. She taught me how to be a good friend to other people who are grieving: just do something to show you care and haven't forgotten them. Send cards, leave flowers at the door, let them know you are ready to go for a walk or go out to lunch or have them over for tea whenever they feel up to it. Keep trying even if you're not getting any response, but gently and respectfully.
>
> Julie Jones, Branson, Missouri

Those of us going through grief have a unique opportunity to bond with those we may barely have known before as they dare to draw close to us in our pain. Conversations that go below the surface can become the foundation for new and deeper friendships that give us strength in the midst of sorrow.

> I wish people would have asked us to do something more often. Many people left us alone, and we figured they were not comfortable with us. It was exhausting for me to try to plan social times and then to have energy to do them. It was the best when friends would ask us to their house, even just for dessert, and would understand if we kept the night short. It

still was nice to get out, and I did not need to find the strength
to clean the house and prepare food.

Kim, Kansas

But we also need to remember that while people don't want to be left alone even if their instinct is to isolate themselves, they do need some alone time.

I wish people had understood that it was okay for me to want
to be alone after the loss of my daughter. I think people were
scared that I would go into a depression or a hermit-like state.
I actually needed to be alone sometimes to pray, to look at her
pictures, and to cry without anyone feeling sorry for me. I also
liked to be alone to watch a funny TV show that I could laugh
at without people judging my laughter as being over my grief.
I needed to be alone to read cards I was sent and immerse
myself in the care and concern of the words of others.

Jamie Crump, Cypress, Texas

Just keep showing up with no agenda. If you are like me, that takes some determined effort—I'm a planner with lots of ideas and lots of insights that I'm quite sure would be helpful. I have to learn more and more to make it my agenda to have no agenda except for showing up and doing my best to shut up.

Finally, oftentimes we don't show up simply because we're afraid. We think, *I will probably do or say something wrong and hurt rather than help.* Honestly, this is always a risk in regard to interacting with hurting people. I often think of grief as being like a burn. When you have a burn on your body and rub up against something, it hurts. You may have bumped and rubbed this part of your body all of the time before and it didn't hurt so the bump or rub was unnoticed. But now, because of the burn, you are especially sensitive. When someone is grieving, the emotional injury is much like the physical injury of a burn. They are far more sensitive to being rubbed the wrong way, to being poked. It takes a lot of courage to approach and linger with someone in this much pain. But when we do—carefully, compassionately, quietly, humbly—the reward is worth the risk. Being used to bring comfort to others is deeply satisfying, even when we don't do it perfectly, or, in our view, sufficiently. So go ahead. Don't let fear of doing the wrong thing keep you from entering in.

4

WHAT TO DO

(AND WHAT NOT TO DO)

Most of us would love to "be there" for those who are grieving. But what does that even look like? Of course, people are all different, so how we offer practical support will slightly differ from one person to the next. But there are some clear commonalities in good ways to do it. Let's look together at what grieving people wish you knew about what it means to show up for them in meaningful ways.

WHAT TO DO WHEN YOU SHOW UP

Listen more than you talk. I know we just spent a whole chapter on what to say and what not to say and now I'm bringing it up again. But it is worth saying again in the "doing" department that one of the best things you can do is simply listen—without interrupting, without correcting, without fixing, without advice-giving, without judging. The truth is, most people process grief through talking. We need to talk about what happened, our fears and frustrations, our memories and our regrets. We need someone who will come alongside us and be comfortable with our confusion and with our need to simply vent the pain that is inside.

> A couple came over the night of the accident, and the only thing they said was "I'm sorry." And then they just sat there. They did not feel the need to talk, ask questions, or try to comfort. They were just *there*. That was comfort. They may have said something during the course of the evening, but they were there to listen, not talk or give advice.
>
> Sharon Smith, Muncie, Indiana

Don't begin to think, when you've been willing to listen, that you haven't really done anything. To be a gracious and generous listener is giving a gift grieving people really need that many people are simply ill-equipped to provide.

> On the day [my daughter] Sarah died, my closest friends acted out Job 2:11–13. They came immediately, stayed as long as I needed them to, joined me in my suffering, and said nothing.
>
> Brian Brinkmann, Weatherford, Texas

> I had three humble and wise friends walking closely with me. They all listened, asked follow-up questions to make sure they were understanding what I meant, and they said little. When they did speak, it was full of appropriate gospel truths, because they had taken the time to understand my unique struggle.
>
> Donna, Texas

One friend of mine didn't say anything although she *listened* as I voiced my memories and irrational thoughts about if I had only given a more perfect gospel presentation, I could be assured that they are with Christ. She didn't judge my anger as inappropriate or selfish. She also didn't judge any of my "if only" statements. I was free to not make sense. I was just free to grieve!

Nicole Gray, Phoenix, Arizona

I see grief as an ocean that brings days with calm waters and sunshine when I relish the sweet memories of my precious son, Cameron. Then, out of nowhere, a rogue wave will hit, or a storm will develop. I just want someone to hang onto the life raft with me while I ride out the waves and storms of grief and wait for the sunshine again.

Tina Guidry Patterson, Nashville, Tennessee

Let it go. As you lean in and listen, be willing to simply let a lot of things go. You don't have to be too quick to examine and reject or correct everything your grieving friend is saying. At least not at first. Lots of questions have to get floated out there. Lots of ideas and assumptions have to get tested. A really good friend lets a lot of things go, especially in the early days of grief. She forgot to call you back. Let it go. They didn't include you. Let it go. He seemed like he didn't even care about what was going on with you. Let it go.

Weep. I don't know where we get the idea that we need to be strong for someone who is grieving and assume we shouldn't weep in their presence. We can be tempted to think that our tears in some way add to the sorrow someone else is feeling. But, in reality, our tears demonstrate to those who are grieving that they are not alone. For so long during my grief, I felt as if I was carrying huge buckets of sorrow everywhere I went, and whenever I saw tears on someone else's face, it felt like they were picking up one of my buckets and carrying it for me. It never added to my sorrow, it just assured me that other people valued Hope and Gabe and demonstrated that their lives mattered.

> It ministered deeply to me when a couple people cried *with* me and were sad *with* me, rather than for me. Those shared tears were worth a thousand words.
>
> Lisa Ellenburg, Winona, Minnesota

> I had a friend who actually told me she was praying for God to allow her to carry some of our grief. She knew there was no way to shoulder what we were going through in the loss of our son, but it was such a precious sentiment that she would want some of that road we were walking.
>
> Melisa Phillips, Nashville, Tennessee

We sometimes resist "bringing it up" because the grieving person seems happy in the moment. He doesn't seem to be thinking about it, and we don't want to "bring him down." But this just isn't the reality. Grief is like a lens or veil through which those going through it see and experience everything. It's like a computer program running in the background at all times. When we speak to a grieving person about the one who died, and they begin to weep, it's not that we "made them cry." Rather, we've acknowledged what was beneath the surface and given them an opportunity to release some of the sadness that was already there.

Laugh. I'll never forget what one woman told me on the second night of our first Respite Retreat after we played a game together. She said, "We haven't laughed out loud since our son died. That felt good."

There are at least two great fears that keep grieving people from laughing around others. First, they're afraid that if they laugh out loud, everyone will think they are now officially "over it" and that no further compassion or care is needed. Second, they're afraid that people around them will think they must not have really loved the one who died if they are able to be so happy. Maybe you don't think these fears make sense or that people should feel this way. But they do.

The reason the parents who come to our retreats are able to laugh together is that by the time we've told our stories and shared many tears and meals together, talking through the agonies of losing a child, we no longer fear that anyone in the room will think we're "over it" or that we didn't really love our child.

We have to earn the right to laugh around or with our grieving friends. We earn that right by being willing to weep with them, by demonstrating and perhaps telling them outright that we are well aware of the load of grief they are carrying and that we don't assume it is going to be dealt with quickly. Perhaps it begins by saying something like, "I know you are so very sad. And I have no interest in rushing you through your sadness. In fact, I want to be there with you in your sadness. But I also figure that sometimes you might appreciate a break from your sadness with someone who won't think that you're officially done with your grief if you laugh. So you just let me know when you're ready to go out to a funny movie or watch something funny on TV together. We'll laugh and hopefully feel better for at least a little while. I'm sure the sadness will be there to pick up again, but I'm with you when you want to take a break from it."

To laugh—really laugh—has tremendous healing power. It relieves the pressure. In fact, laughter actually increases the flow of endorphins, our body's naturally produced painkiller. To laugh is to take a mini-vacation from the pain of loss. And sometimes when you are so, so sad, you really wish you could put that sorrow on the shelf for just a day, just an hour, just a minute, and feel good.

> There were people who said things like, "I am going to come pick you up for book club." They knew better than to ask me if I wanted to go, and they knew I still needed to live. I am thankful to all those who helped me continue to live and those who kept me laughing, which was invaluable. I desperately needed to laugh with people who knew that when I laughed, it didn't mean I wasn't sad.
>
> Rachel Anderson, College Station, Texas

> All the kind words and loving hugs got to be way, way too much for my introverted, grieving self. I knew people were just being loving, but oh my stars! I couldn't bear it. So it helped me greatly when close friends, real friends whom I knew I could call 24/7, who definitely expressed concern for me let me just *live life*, not constantly talking about my mom or the death or funeral or whatever. I needed *some* degree of normalcy, and I was glad for the interactions/conversations/emails that weren't only about this sad thing. It was a grace, and I needed it.
>
> Tara Barthel, Billings, Montana

Leave a message. These days with texting and email and social media, people are talking on the phone less and less. In the best of days, many people just don't want to answer or talk on the phone. In the midst of grief it can be a huge chore to answer the phone; it might mean getting caught in an awkward conversation or being asked questions you just don't want to answer. But that doesn't mean you don't want people to call. To be able to listen (and maybe listen again) to a genuine, kind, undemanding message left by someone who simply wants to check in and express that they care is a great gift. So call. And if the grieving person doesn't answer, don't just hang up; leave a message. And be sure to include in the message, "Feel no need to call me back."

> I appreciated it when people left prayers on my voicemail.
>> Helen Silva, Modesto, California

If you're someone who is close enough to be at the grieving person's house right after her loved one has died, it is a great gift to find a pad of paper and start answering the phone and checking messages, keeping very good notes of who calls and what is being offered or what is needed. It can be so hard for the grieving person to keep telling the same story over and over again and such a great relief to have a friend who can be trusted to do that on her behalf.

Send a note, and then another. I have never been much of a note writer. I'm still not that good at it. But on this side of grief, I'm better than I used to be. Before our experience of loss, I never knew that a simple card or note—someone putting pen to paper to enter into sorrow—could mean so much to someone who is hurting. But day by day David and I would go to the mailbox and find it full of tangible expressions of love. I'm weeping now as I remember how we would come inside the house, sit on the front stairs, read the letters, and not feel so alone as we did the hardest thing we had ever done—keep on living after our child died.

The first thing I ever wrote for publication after Hope died was a little article I called "The Worst Thing to Say to Someone Who's Grieving . . . Nothing." In that article, written in the midst of the daily ritual of receiving and reading cards, I wrote:

> Recently I went out and bought a packet of blank cards with beautiful pictures so I'll have cards on hand to send when I need them. I've learned that it doesn't matter if the card has the perfect picture or sentiment on it. What matters is what is written inside and that it gets sent, no matter how much time it takes.
>
> In fact, to be truthful, I barely read what is printed on the card, but I soak in every word that is written personally and often go back and reread them.

My friend Sue is the best note writer I've ever known. I have a file folder full of notes I've received from her over the years, as birthdays and deathdays and other hard days have come and gone. And the other day I talked to her and her husband, Dan, as they are grieving the loss of their adult son, Mark. Dan said, "Every day we go out to the mailbox, and we find letters—some from people we don't know, but they knew Mark. And they tell us stories about him we haven't heard. We sit and read through them together and then go back and reread them."

Some people seem to have a gift for writing notes. For others of us, it takes more of an effort, more of a decision to just do it.

About six weeks after the death of my mother, a friend that I had not heard from regarding her death sent me a card telling me that she had bought the card right after my mom's death and kept it in a highly visible spot in her house as a reminder to continue to pray for me. It meant a lot to know that even after the dust had settled, so to speak, that friend had continued to uphold me.

Pam, Pennsylvania

I appreciated friends and family who sent multiple cards. I knew they weren't just checking a box on the socially acceptable things to do for someone who has experienced a loss but were actually thinking of us. Not that others weren't; it's just we knew for sure these folks were.

Heather Etner, Vienna, Virginia

Mark your calendar. It is good to send a card immediately upon someone's death. But here's what is even better—to send another note a month later, at the three-month, the six-month, and the one-year mark. And you probably can't rely on your memory to make that happen. So when you get the email that tells you about someone's loss, take a minute to note those milestones on your calendar so you can drop a note or send an email or text, letting him know you remember. Throughout the year, you might keep a list of people who have lost their mother or father so that you can send them a note on their first Mother's Day or Father's Day without that parent. You might keep a list of people who lose their spouse so that you can send them a note on Valentine's Day or at Christmas to let them know you're remembering how they might feel the void especially on that day. You might keep a list of people who have lost loved ones throughout the year and send a note as New Year's Eve approaches, letting them know that you understand it must be hard to anticipate hearing "Happy New Year!" when thinking about the new year without the person they love makes them so very sad.

It is also good to remember that for most grieving people, it is the days leading up to the birthdate, deathdate, or other notable date that are actually harder than the day itself. So it is a sweet thing to let them know you are thinking of them as the day approaches and ask if there is any way you could help to make that day easier.

A simple text or email sent to a bereaved person on the birthday of a loved one and the anniversary of his or her death goes a long way in letting a grieving parent, spouse, or sibling know that his or her deceased family member is still remembered and cherished. You can program your cell phone calendar app with these important dates one time only and have it remind you indefinitely. When life gets crazy, you will have a helpful reminder regarding both dates each and every year. Just one text can make a huge difference in comforting a bereaved person on these especially difficult days.

Le Ann Trees, San Diego, California

Remembering the "firsts" after a friend's loss is a wonderfully sensitive way to show kindness. The first Christmas, the first birthday, the first Mother's Day, the first anniversary of their death . . . these are big events to someone who is grieving. When someone takes time to acknowledge them, it is a tremendous gift.

Beth, Minnesota

I have a very dear friend who is so thoughtful and compassionate. On Abby's fifth "birthday" (the day she was stillborn), Stephanie sent me a card with a gift certificate for a massage.

On Abby's tenth "birthday," she sent me a gift certificate to our favorite restaurant. On both occasions, she wrote in the card she gave us that we should be celebrating our daughter's birthday and that Abby was very special to her also though she never met her. Sometimes our own family forgets Abby's birthday; Stephanie hasn't missed one year. On a day that I am feeling down, I am so blessed to have a friend who picks me up.

Jaimie Crump, Cypress, Texas

A candle and a note were put in my mailbox after what would have been my daughter's ten-year high school reunion with a note saying that they remembered their friends that had passed away during their senior year of high school and that she was not forgotten.

Mary Ellen Ashworth, Fayetteville, Georgia

It's helpful and kind when people acknowledge our sadness during transitional times or special moments such as the start of school, senior picture time, sports seasons, prom, birthdays, family vacations taken without the whole family, events that we no longer need to attend, and other milestones that our child would've hit. When a friend of mine was at her daughter's senior photo shoot, she texted me with a thoughtful message about how she recognized that I would not get to have this experience with my son, and she hurt for me in the midst of her joy that day. Because of her care for my sad heart and the way she wept with me, I was then better able to enter into her special moment and rejoice with her.

Jodi Blick, Omaha, Nebraska

A woman from our church who gave birth in another hospital at the time of Joshua's death sent us a card shortly after the first

Easter after Joshua's death that said she and her family were remembering precious Joshua. She also sent us another card saying she remembers Joshua as her son celebrates his birthdays. I guess it was more who this was from rather than what she said. Some people are in a unique position to bless others.

Heather Etner, Vienna, Virginia

As we approached the first anniversary of Al's death, someone commented that we must be relieved to see an end to all the "firsts" without Al. But I found that I didn't want to be done with the firsts. They were painful, but the acute pain of missing and remembering Al on each occasion had the effect of linking us intimately with him. It was like floating down a river, passing signs marking "X amount of time since Al's death." The reminders of his absence were sad, but they still connected us to the event that initiated them—his death. Once we reached the end of the firsts, we would leave the familiarity of the river and be propelled into the big, shoreless sea of "the rest of our lives." Sure, we would continue to mark time and to celebrate birthdays and holidays, but it would all be part of "life after Al" in a nebulous way that would stretch into countless years. That was a different kind of hard.

Libby Groves[12]

Go through your photos. One of the hard things about losing someone you love is that over time, you realize your most vivid memories of that person are becoming more limited to those you have actual pictures of. You won't ever get a chance to take new, fresh pictures. But when someone gives you a photograph of your loved one that you don't have, it is like getting a little bit of that person back. It brings a fresh sense of enjoying the person you love again.

So go through your photos and look for photos of the deceased that his or her family might not have and make a copy for them. And if you come across one later and think too much time has passed for it to matter, you're wrong! It will be all the more welcome.

One of my son's friends forwarded a quote from my son that was in a yearbook from when he was in the eighth grade. Several other friends sent digital photos of themselves with Brady. These were so special because I had never seen them.

Jeanne Pierce, San Antonio, Texas

Bring stuff. We all think food when we try to come up with something to take to a grieving family. And food is good! But sometimes food can become a burden. It is not a blessing to have rotting food on the counter that you feel guilty throwing away. And it is not a blessing to run out of space in your refrigerator or freezer for everything being brought to you. So when you're taking food, consider carefully how many people are in the house. Consider the reality that many people lose their appetite in the midst of grief. Consider making your gift the organization of food gifts from others who are anxious to help so that the food deliveries get spread out over a period of time, perhaps by setting up a Take-Them-A-Meal online calendar.[13] Don't assume that your gift of a meal is somehow less thoughtful if you don't cook it yourself. Most families these days find a meal bought from a restaurant and delivered to their door a real treat, especially when they are not up to going out in public to get it. Consider giving them a gift card for a restaurant that delivers so they can get what they want when they want it. Find out what restaurants the family enjoys and what they like to order and pass that information along to others who want to help.

Take whatever food you make in a disposable container so they don't have to track you down to return it. Include a DVD they might enjoy watching after dinner and a note with a pleasant memory about the person who died that they might enjoy sharing together over dinner. If there are children in the family, find out what food they love (and what mom and dad love to feed them) and make that part of the meal you deliver. Go by the house sometime and offer to take the kids out for burgers or ice cream.

Somewhere along the way, as people brought us meals in the midst of our grief, I began asking them to bring enough for themselves too and to stay and eat with us. I'm quite sure that dinner guests would not be a "gift" to some people and to some families. But it was to us. We had sweet, memorable conversations around the table and got to know people we never would have set up a social engagement with otherwise. But whether or not you offer or are invited to stay, remember that your visit is half of the gift. So make it a gift and not an additional burden.

And of course there are things besides food you can bring to the house:

Two of my friends brought food over, but with it they brought toilet paper, paper plates, and cups. The toilet paper was what actually was the most meaningful. At that point I was so overwhelmed that I wasn't thinking straight, so they were thinking for me. Other friends came over the next morning and cleaned my house so I was ready for family coming in from out of town.

JoAnne Riker, Gallatin, Tennessee

They brought us some daily necessities that you're not thinking about, like toilet paper, paper plates, a big bag of coffee.
Simple things that help you get through those first couple of
weeks.

Brandon and Carol Trujillo, Santa Clarita, California

There was a ton of food brought to my home after the death
of my husband. But the gift I remember most was a grocery
sack of paper products (plates, napkins, cups, plastic serving utensils). It was useful and saved a lot of sinks overloaded
with dishes since there were lots of extra people around.

Lois Horsens, Florence, Montana

People brought over not just food for us, but dog food for our
two dogs.

Jordan, Washington State

A friend gave me a manicure before the funeral. Another made
an appointment for me to get my hair done. These things
made me feel so cared for.

Kathy Howarter

The church where my sister's husband serves as a pastor
stocked my sister's refrigerator with food when they were
at the funeral for my mom so that they came home to a full
fridge. A number of members of the church that I pastor drove
five hours to be at the memorial service. This outpouring of
love was extremely comforting to us.

Nick Batzig, Richmond Hill, Georgia

As important as is all this support surrounding the funeral, it
is important to remember that the really hard times come in the
days and weeks and months after the funeral, when everything

gets quiet and the grieving are beginning to wonder if everyone has forgotten them and their loss.

A lot of people were super helpful leading up to the funeral. Then after the funeral people expect you to be able to start moving on with your life. In many ways things get much harder after the funeral, yet that's when others move on—not because they don't care, but because they don't realize how hard it still is.

Kassandra, Texas

You may not know how much power you have to bless grieving people with kindness. I am moved and amazed by the creative ways people find to bless those who are grieving. Maybe you'll find an idea or two from what these grieving people found meaningful:

My daughter-in-law made a CD especially for me, composed of different songs that were encouraging. They acknowledged and validated my grief and loss while giving me hope for the future. Three years later I still listen to that CD, and it reminds me of how far I've come in my journey.

Claybra Selmon, Tampa, Florida

One friend helped me make a children's book for my girls when they were toddlers about their grandma in heaven.

Melissa, Gainesville, Florida

One of my daughter's friends made stars for the funeral so people could write a memory or Scripture or something to encourage us. After the funeral they put all the stars in a beautiful box and gave it to us. I didn't look at them for a long time but every now and then I will pull out that box and be encouraged.

Vicki Font, Ontario, Canada

When my mom died, my daughter's teacher knitted me a prayer shawl. She said she prayed for me while she knitted it and told me when I wore it to remember I was covered in prayer.

Michelle Buck, Woodbury, Minnesota

Someone planted trees in a national park in my son's memory; I was so touched to think something would live on for hundreds of years because of him.

Robin Tierney, Massapequa, New York

On a gift to our stillborn daughter, friends wrote her name: "We love you Evangeline Joy xoxo." To me, those words validated her as a person and validated our loss. A dear friend put in the time and effort to create a memory book for our stillborn daughter and included verses, poems, and insights that have been especially meaningful to us.

Laura Hoevenaars, Whitby, Ontario, Canada

One friend took flowers from the arrangements at the memorial service and had them preserved in a paperweight, not only for me, but also for my mom and my sister. She also had bookmarks made for other family members—people she did not even know.

Catha Jaynes, Houston, Texas

After things had settled down, a friend accompanied me to a "spa day." That meant a lot. I needed a break and didn't want to be alone.

Doris, Ontario, Canada

When Valentine's Day came around five months after Samuel went to heaven, dear friends organized everyone from church and our community to fill our mailbox with messages of love and encouragement. They all used green hearts, since Samuel had a mitochondrial disorder, and that's the color for awareness. What a precious gift it was and still is over a year and a half later!

Mary Elisabeth Cutliff, Anderson, South Carolina

A friend of mine is an accomplished seamstress. She had the idea to take some of Savannah's clothes and make a quilt out of them. We now have it hanging in our house as a reminder of our sweet girl.

Ashley Sinclair, Greenville, South Carolina

My husband and I were given several gifts of date nights and free babysitting. It showed me that others valued helping to strengthen our marriage in the midst of losing our daughter.

Laura Hoevenaars, Whitby, Ontario, Canada

An Easter lily and/or Christmas poinsettia given in our daughter's memory continues to mean a lot these many years later.

Eunice, Alabama

Someone took forty encouraging and comforting verses of Scripture and inserted my name into the appropriate places, printed them out on cardstock, and mounted them to pretty scrapbook paper. Another group of ladies made a quilt for me out of my husband's clothing. One gal from church drove out to my house (twenty minutes from her home) and picked up my laundry twice a week for the entire summer after my husband's death. One friend, who lives a distance away, sent monthly care packages of snacks and goodies for the kids and me for the first year. Another friend did all my Christmas shopping and gift-wrapping that first Christmas. My husband had been dead six months by that point, but she knew I was still feeling overwhelmed.

Sarah Heywood, Swan, Iowa

Our church community gave us a collection of cards and small gifts, one a day for forty days. The individual or family who supplied the card or gift for that day also committed to pray for us that day. The recurring, visible, tangible reminder that we were not alone was incredibly helpful and humbling.

Carola, Brant County, Ontario

Even now, years later, I have a friend who brings pink cup-cakes over every year on Selah's birthday. Those small things that let us know her life is remembered—they are beautiful reminders of God's love.

Kara Chupp, Portland, Oregon

Our small group arranged for a flight and beautiful hotel with everything paid for to somewhere warm and beautiful for just my husband and me. They arranged for my parents to be in town to watch our other children and made reservations for everything. It was a time for my husband and me to breathe and reconnect a few months after Isaac's death. What a loving sacrifice.

Melisa Phillips, Nashville, Tennessee

My dear aunt sent a letter notifying us that she had purchased a small goat through the Heifer Project. I know it sounds funny, yet she knew what we who loved him knew: Andy loved animals. He rescued and adopted animals. Knowing this little goat would be providing milk to small children just seemed the perfect way to honor him.

Coley Fisher, Brea, California

I ordered a copy of my son's favorite childhood book with the intention of donating it to our public library in his memory. I've done this for several years to commemorate a happy occasion, such as a birthday or a graduation, in honor of my son. The woman who ordered it paid for it instead of giving me a bill and sent me a color copy of the book's cover with a picture of the sticker inside that said it was given in my son's memory. Wow.

Robin Tierney, Massapequa, New York

My dear friend gave me a gift certificate to a local nursery to choose whatever I wanted to remember my dad.

Jeri, Iowa

Instead of giving me books my friend thought would be good for me (which probably would not have been), she asked me what books I found helpful. Then she bought them, read them, and asked me what parts were the most significant to me. This was her loving way to really try to understand my sadness and to share it with me.

Kim, Kansas

It means so much when people visit the cemetery and let us know that they were there by sending us a picture or a thoughtful gift. A dear friend welded together a beautiful metal cross in his workshop and placed it out at our son's graveside. We were deeply touched by his thoughtfulness and initiative.

Jodi Blick, Omaha, Nebraska

Pay for stuff. Death is expensive. Even though no amount of money can bring back the deceased or make the hurt go away, providing financial help with the many expenses that surround a death is a significant and meaningful way to bless someone going through the most difficult thing they've ever experienced. They will never forget it. What might you offer to pay for?

- Funeral home services
- Casket
- Grave plot
- Gravestone
- Honorarium to pastor conducting the service
- Honorarium to musicians who help with the service
- Anything that would add to the service (recently I helped to arrange for a bagpipe player to play at the graveside service of a young man who went to a college where bagpipes are often played. It was the perfect way for the college to contribute to the service in a way that really blessed not only this young man's fellow students, but also the family and other mourners.)
- Airfare or other expenses for traveling to a loved one's funeral
- Hotel expenses for family members who come in town for the funeral
- Portrait, photographic, or video services for the service
- A new suit or dress for the funeral
- A week or weekend away at the beach or in the mountains
- Babysitting for the children too young to be at the visitation or funeral
- Babysitting for counseling or GriefShare sessions
- A weekend or weeklong getaway at a cabin, at the beach, in the mountains
- Grief counseling

We had a friend who watched our youngest son while we went to our fifty-eight counseling sessions. She refused to let us pay her too.

Jamie, St. Louis, Missouri

My sisters took my two young daughters to the mall on the day we were to make funeral arrangements for my son. They picked out a few outfits for me to choose from for the girls to wear to his memorial service. They also picked some clothing for me. It was a huge help not to have to shop for those outfits, and they just returned the ones I did not choose.

Melissa Spiceland, Vinton, Virginia

Invite but don't push. For some mysterious reason I've never been able to put my finger on, facing a crowd when you're grieving can be hard. Walking into church, a Little League game, a popular restaurant, a mall, and other places can be emotionally overwhelming. You know that people you might encounter are very afraid of saying the wrong thing or dread the possibility that things will get awkward. I remember in those early months that I headed to church each week with two significant fears. I was afraid that everyone would ask me about Hope. And I was afraid no one would speak to me about Hope. Both possibilities made each Sunday hard for a long time.

People wanted to reach out and draw us into the conversation of everyday life. But I could not yet enter that conversation. People were passing pasta and talking about vacations and I could hardly breathe.

Gregory Floyd [14]

I wish people who are grieving would get a social pass. It's hard to attend things. Grief is not a topic for small talk. You find yourself lying and saying you are just fine or breaking down and embarrassed by your inability to control your emotions.

Catha Jaynes, Houston, Texas

I wish people would understand when I cancel at the last minute. My grief is new and raw. I would love to attend your party, and when you invite me three weeks in advance, at that moment I really, really want to attend, but I never know how I will feel when it's party time.

Robin Tierney, Massapequa, New York

It really meant a lot to us that we had someone who would save us the back pew at church so we could slip in and slip out more easily.

Melissa Joy, Elk, Washington

Our compassion and willingness to reach out and include others as well as be sensitive to the difficulty of social situations for those who are grieving grows as we seek to put ourselves in their shoes and imagine how the death of the person they love has changed everything. If you are married, think for a minute about how difficult it must be to go from always having a companion at every event to always walking in alone. Allow that growing empathy to prompt you to invite those who have lost a spouse to start sitting with you in church or going to lunch with you on Sundays. Ask them over to play cards on Friday night. Keep including them in events that they used to take part in with their spouse.

One of the most difficult things for couples who lose a child is to attend events such as baby showers, graduations, school programs, ball games, and weddings of their child's friends. Oftentimes, especially when the grief is new, they likely won't have the energy or the courage to do it. But they do want to be invited, even if they can't come. And they want others to recognize the difficulty in it for them. Life for a bereaved parent presents a steady stream of events to celebrate for other people's children that they will never celebrate for their own child. Some parents find comfort attending these kinds of events, as being around their child's friends brings their deceased child close. For others, such events are an overwhelming reminder of what they've lost, and they just can't do it. Or sometimes they just can't do it yet.

No one seemed to recognize how hard a baby shower might be for me. No one offered to buy the gift for me, sit with me, hold my hand, and be my "wingman." That would have helped.

Melissa, Gainesville, Florida

Having lost our baby in the womb, I was thankful when a friend who was hosting a baby shower for another friend invited me and made me feel welcome to attend but no pressure if I wasn't ready.

Laura Hoevenaars, Whitby, Ontario, Canada

I remember when parents' night at my son's school rolled around shortly after Hope's death. It just felt so hard to face that crowd. I felt like I had "that woman whose baby died" emblazoned across my forehead. It really helped that a friend made a point to connect with me and offer to meet me at the door so that I knew I had a safe person at my side.

Grieving people often feel that they don't fit in anymore. Social events that used to be fun can now feel like a burden. But they need the gentle encouragement to return to life with friends and life as part of the body of Christ, both serving and being served. Even though they don't come for a while, keep inviting. Figure out how to make it easy for them to walk in the door and understand when they wear out quickly and go home early. Ask them what would make it easier for them and then do what you can.

> When there was a big social gathering or community event, it meant so much to get a call from a friend asking (1) if we were up for going, could they pick us up or meet us there so that we wouldn't have to walk in alone or sit by ourselves? And (2) if we weren't up for going, asking if we would like to come to their house for dinner instead, or if it would be helpful for them to stop by our house to pray or visit. It meant so much to know that they were willing to miss out on a fun event like a football game, parade, or party in order to help us by entering into our grief and do what would speak love to us instead.
>
> Eric and Jodi Blick, Omaha, Nebraska

> People arranged for my kids to be taken to and from school events that we could not bring ourselves to attend.
>
> Sharon Smith, Muncie, Indiana

Consider the kids. There's a lot that I haven't figured out in regard to helping kids through grief, but one thing is clear: mostly kids just want things to be normal. All the weird upset in schedule, people in the house, people crying, putting a body in the ground, unfamiliar food brought by strangers—it is all unwelcome and uncomfortable to most kids. And then there are the questions—questions about how they feel and what they think that they just don't have vocabulary to express. They don't want to be the kid whose dad or mom or sibling died. They don't want to be anything other than like everybody else. They crave the old routine. So if you are in a position to help maintain the routine, be it mealtime, soccer practice, piano lessons, favorite TV show, Boy Scouts, or bedtime ritual, that can be a great way to serve the family.

> What I remember most about the funeral process was all these old people crowding around me who would see me and start crying. They would ask me questions and I didn't know what to say. It was all very awkward. I just wanted to be alone with my family and my mom. It took me a long time to realize that my dad was never coming back. It just didn't sink in for a few weeks. There were so many people at our house all the time, and a part of me thought that maybe if they left we'd start to get back to normal, and then he'd come back. What I wanted most was for things to go back to being normal again.
>
> Rachel Robbins Ferrell, Chattanooga, Tennessee[15]

Oftentimes kids do have a sense that they can't really talk to their parents or parent about their sadness, fear, or anger, because Mom or Dad is already so on edge, so burdened with sorrow. To be willing to develop a relationship, get on the floor and play, swing by in the car to take them to play at the park, and be a safe person for the children to talk to are great gifts to the family.

Be patient. Sometimes I think we're in a much bigger hurry than God is for people to get better. Just as time is one element in the healing of a physical injury, so time is one element in the healing of the deep wound of losing someone we love. But we have ways of subtly communicating to grieving people that we wish they would hurry up with this grief thing and get back to being the fun-loving, interesting people they were before.

> Please be patient and don't expect me to have my same vibrancy, energy and drive that I once did. But don't give up on me. I need to know you accept me where I'm at and will walk next to me until I return again to my "ole self." And please be okay with the fact that I am changed forever. I hope to be the way God meant me to be. I want to be transformed through this pain. Please pray for me to that end.
>
> Dena McGoldrick, Clinton Township, Michigan

Our desire for the grieving to feel better is sometimes purely out of love, not wanting them to have to continue to feel the pain they are feeling now. But other times, there may be a bit of selfishness in our desire for them to get better. Sad people are really not much fun to be with. We get tired of always having to consider their sensitivities and energy level. We get tired of everything always being so hard.

> The hardest part of my grieving came six months down the road when I was weary and tired, and it seemed as if others were expecting me to move on and be over it.
>
> Beth Gowing, Montreal, Quebec, Canada

Letting grieving friends know that as much as you desire for the load of grief to be lessened in their life, you have no intention of rushing them through it, nor will you insist that they get back "to normal" on your timetable. This is a great gift of friendship. To be a patient friend over the long haul of grief requires a lot of dying to self and serving another.

> You may think I looked so together at the funeral. It wasn't for eight weeks until I really let go. And then I cried a cry that I didn't even recognize.
>
> Nancy (Moran) Skilbred, Oakdale, Minnesota

> So many well-meaning people wanted to push us over the hump and move us to the joy and the hope that is ours in Christ in the midst of grief. And whether intentionally or unintentionally, we were sometimes made to feel that the lingering of our grief was a sign of spiritual immaturity. Now, however, with years of hindsight to glean from, I praise God that He did not remove the pain that laid heavy on our hearts when we pleaded for it but waited until the fruit it was producing was fully grown.
>
> Angela Taylor, Dallas, Texas

Help with funds and causes. These days we often read that in lieu of flowers, donations may be made to particular organizations or causes in memory of the person who died. Don't underestimate how much you can touch someone who is grieving by your monetary gift to a cause that the deceased cared about. And if you're not sure that the grieving ones will be notified of your gift, don't hesitate to drop them a note telling them how much joy it gave you to contribute in that person's memory and why. They want to know that the person they love is being honored in this way. They want to hear why you were motivated to give.

These days, funds and causes tend to continue long past the funeral of the person who died. Many grieving people feel not just a desire but also some societal pressure to "carry on" their loved one's memory or passion by hosting a run to raise money for disease research, organizing an annual toy drive for the hospital where their child was treated, or pursing some other project in memory of the deceased. Know that your participation in these funds, causes, and events is a tangible way to come alongside and share in their joy of seeing something good come out of something so difficult.

Offer to help with the hard stuff. Everything feels hard in the midst of grief—especially anything that reminds you of the person you've lost and the change in your life because of the loss. And pretty much everything reminds you of that.

> It felt odd that the reality of Al's death was not patently obvious to everyone I came into contact with. I felt as if I had lost a leg or had half my face burned away; surely my loss was as visible on the outside as it was on the inside. Yet when I was pumping gas or grocery shopping, strangers around me were totally unaware of the ache in my chest or that anything was amiss.
>
> Libby Groves[16]

Going to the grocery store reminds you of what you don't have to buy anymore because the loved one you lost is not in the house. Everywhere you go reminds you of conversations and experiences. It's hard to find the energy or initiative to get the exercise you know you need. Crowds of people are hard. But things get a little bit easier when a friend comes alongside to help.

My friend Angela moved to a new house about a year after her husband died. She had never had the strength to go through her husband's closet and belongings to figure out what she wanted to keep and what she wanted to give away. And she still didn't have the strength to do it as moving day approached. So our mutual friend Paul Riviere (yes, that's really his name, and he's awesome!) rented a storage unit and went to her house and basically moved everything from the closet to the storage unit. She didn't have to deal with it when it was already so very hard to be moving to a new home without her husband.

In the deaths of my children, I have had to do so many hard things that I never imagined I would have to do. Having a friend at my side has always made hard things a little bit easier. Perhaps you need to ask your grieving friend what hard thing they need to do but don't know how to do, or can't find the strength to do, and offer to do it for her or with her. Here are some hard things you might offer to do:

- Pick out and deliver clothes for the deceased to be buried in
- Plan the memorial service
- Clean out the closet and take some things to be donated or distributed
- Pick out and order the casket or gravestone
- Put together a scrapbook, slideshow, or video
- Decorate for Christmas
- Write and address thank-you notes
- Get the deceased's home or property ready to sell
- Redo the will or adjust financial plans and papers

When I returned from my mother's funeral, which was out of state, I brought back a box of some of her things that I wanted to keep. I couldn't bring myself to look through the box for several months. When I was ready to open it, I called a friend who came over and sat with me on the floor. She let me pull out things one by one and talk about my memories of my mom and how I missed her. My friend gave me the gift of her presence, which I've never forgotten. I praise God for her sensitivity and caring.

Donna Tyree, Columbia City, Indiana

One of the best ways you can help a grieving friend is to offer to go with him to do the hard things. So consider offering to go along to the morgue, the funeral home, the cemetery, the grave, the grocery store, church, a school event, a party, or a vacation.

An out-of-town friend would visit me every few weeks and take me out for lunch. She always asked if I wanted to go to the cemetery and visit Rob's gravesite. I appreciated that so much, to have her to stand there with me, talk about Rob, life, death, heaven, and even not to talk, just to stand there and be there with me. No other friends ever asked.

Rachel Andrea, Cape Breton, Canada

Our son was a talented artist and graphic designer who battled anxiety, depression, and addiction. My friends met us at the emergency room at 2:45 a.m. Others met us at our home after we left the ER. They then asked our permission to go to his cabin and clean up the broken glass from the night before. Each step, they asked permission. One dear friend gathered his art and scanned several pieces. Others began to work on the things we would need to get through the day. They continued a care plan that we had in place for a year.

Cindy Blom, Fairview, Tennessee

Commit to being there over the long haul. Most grievers will tell you they got a lot of support surrounding the funeral and for a week or two after. Then it seemed that everyone returned to normal life and no longer came around, no longer brought it up, no longer assumed any help was needed. What grieving people really need is a few friends who make it clear that they intend to show up and help out, not just in an initial spurt of effort but over the long haul.

Of course, you don't want to make any promises you can't keep, thereby adding to the grieving person's sense of loss, but a specific commitment to fill in a gap can provide a sense of security and relieve a host of fears. What needs are weighing heavily on the grieving person about which he or she may feel uncomfortable asking for help? Can you help? Or better yet, could you organize a team of people to help?

An elderly widow might not be able to drive. Offer to take her to church each week or to provide a weekly grocery shopping excursion. You probably won't be able to meet all her transportation needs, but perhaps you could commit to help out once a week or once a month, recruiting others to help once a month as well.

A widower might have rarely done the grocery shopping or prepared his own meals. In addition to inviting him to your house for the occasional meal, perhaps you could involve him in some shopping and food preparation to help him become more self-sufficient.

Parents who have lost a child don't want their sadness to cast a shadow in their home on their other children. But they need some time and space to talk and simply be sad. Perhaps you could offer childcare so the couple can have a once-a-month date night.

Those who were long-term caregivers for a loved one can find themselves hardly knowing what to do with a day that doesn't include patient care routines. Perhaps you could schedule with them a regular date for coffee, walking, or watching a favorite TV show.

> I had friends who pressed in. When I didn't have it in me to ask for help, they kept showing up to listen, encourage, and remind me of truths I didn't want to believe at the time.
>
> Allison Hucks, Nashville, Tennessee

Perhaps about now you're beginning to feel tired at the very thought of showing up for your grieving friend to do all this hard stuff over the long haul. This is probably a good time to mention that you don't have to be—in fact, probably cannot and should not be—the entire support system for someone who is grieving. At its best, nurturing a grieving person back to joy is a community project.

In fact, one of the best things you can do is to help your grieving friend discover and develop a new community of people who are comfortable with grief. One way you can do this is by helping your friend to find and attend a GriefShare group. GriefShare is an incredible ministry to grieving people that centers on weekly small-group meetings at local churches around the country and internationally. When your friend attends a GriefShare group, he or she will be surrounded by others who are working their way through grief too—people who understand the tears and fears, the angst and anger, the questions and frustrations of grief. It can be such an unexpected and welcome relief just to be surrounded by people who get it. GriefShare provides a safe place and an appropriate outlet to keep talking about the person who died long after other friends may have tired of it. At each meeting attendees watch a brief video that offers biblical wisdom and insight from both experts and ordinary people that help to keep them moving forward toward healing and joy.

Because David and I are on the GriefShare videos, people often recognize us in public and come up to us to tell us how much they were helped by the program. The phrase we hear most often is, "GriefShare saved my life." Often they tell us they were hesitant to go at first but ended up repeating the thirteen-week program multiple times, as they were able to hear and process more of what is presented as time went on. They tell us how the members of the group began to minister to each other and became friends. And many of them tell us that they have gone from attending GriefShare to facilitating a GriefShare group.

You might want to help your friend by doing the initial research on groups available in your area.[17] Over thirteen thousand churches around the country and internationally have been equipped to offer GriefShare, so it is likely that a number of groups will pop up when you do the search. Your friend or family member might be reluctant to attend initially. And I get that, don't you? When you're in so much pain, the idea of spending the evening with other people who are in as much pain as you are doesn't sound like it will help at all. It can sound like a recipe for awkward and uncomfortable interactions. You might offer to go with your friend the first time or two until he gets comfortable with it. Some groups will allow you to attend the actual session. Others will ask you to return at a designated time to pick up your friend. Policies vary by group, so check ahead of time. The day may come when your friend says that the best thing you did in the hardest time of his life was to help him attend a GriefShare group.

Point them to Christ. When our friends begin to pour out their confusion in the midst of grief, what comes naturally to many of us is to give them advice. It's one of the characteristics of friendship; we share with one another ideas and solutions that have helped us with our own problems. We want to save our hurting friends with a solution.

But there is something they need much more than our suggestions and solutions. They need the wisdom and knowledge, the perspective and peace, that cannot be found apart from Christ. They need the deep companionship that can be found only in communion with Christ. They need to discover the treasure that has come to them wrapped in a package they never wanted. They need to experience the power and presence of God like never before, perhaps because they never knew how much they needed it before.

None of us can make life work apart from the grace of Christ. Perhaps the person who is grieving has never been desperate enough to have to learn what it means to abide in Christ, depend upon Christ, and rest in Christ. Don't rob her of the opportunity to press into Christ by seeking to fill up every hole and solve every problem yourself. In the loneliness of grief, remind her of the friend who is closer than a brother, the Spirit who dwells within her, the Paraclete, the comforter, the one who brings to mind God's Word which has been planted in her heart.

One of the most encouraging things for me were my three girlfriends Pam, Alyson, and Julie, who committed to meet

with me every Thursday morning for as long as I needed
them. More than the studying of the Word, which I knew I
needed, it was the knowledge that they were going to be
there no matter what.

Jennifer, Louisiana

Perhaps you haven't had a friendship up to this point that
has included praying together over more than a meal. Now is
the time to begin to pray together more personally. Will you get
down on your knees together and beg God to do a healing work
in your friend's broken heart? Are you the friend who will organize a regular prayer group made up of those who recognize
that grief will take some time?

Rather than simply saying, "I will pray for you" in the midst
of the conversation, why not take a moment right there in the
church hallway, in the middle of the grocery store, or wherever
you run into a person who is grieving and say, "Can I pray for
you right now?" In this way you can enter into the presence of
the one person who has the power to bring deep healing and
profound comfort that no one else can. Ask God to meet this
person in the loneliest of times, to make his presence known
and felt. Ask him to provide clarity for the confusion of grief,
patience for the healing process, grace to extend to others who
say hurtful things, perspective about what has happened, and
hopefulness for facing the future. Your willingness to pray in
the moment rather than promise to pray in some unknown future time will create a holy moment of genuine caring.

You may have some good advice for coping with all the
changes and challenges that come with the death of a loved one,
but don't give your advice as though it is the savior your grieving friend needs most. Rather, point him to the Savior.

One friend told me recently that she has an alarm on her phone as a reminder to pray for me every day. This made me feel so loved and cared for! When someone says, "I'll be praying for you," I don't know if that means two times or twelve times or once a week, or, really, if they will remember at all. But to know that I have one friend who spends a few moments every day praying for me—and I know she does, because she has an alarm set for that purpose—that makes me feel remembered and cared for.

Jamie Lorenz, Spokane Valley, Washington

5

Social Media and Grief

(When the "Like" Button

Just Seems Wrong)

In previous generations there were established conventions for offering condolences to the grieving as well as accepted ways of expressing grief. But we are living in a new era—the era of blogs, email, and social media. Most people these days—especially those of the younger generation—would much rather text than talk. We can barely remember the last time we wrote a letter by hand and had to actually find the person's address and a stamp and put it in the mail. We live in an era of instant communication and public sharing of every event in our lives.

So it makes sense that we would also share our great sorrows online for all of the world to see. In fact, those who might never talk in person about their grief will sometimes write about it on a blog or Facebook page. They are more comfortable sharing it that way and perhaps more comfortable receiving expressions of caring that way too.

> I process the world and life through words, so that's what I did. I journaled. I blogged. I wrote long, sappy emails. It was nice of people—especially my nonverbal friends—to bear with me.
>
> Tara Barthel, Billings, Montana

I've tried to figure out what drives me to post something about my children when their birthdays or deathdays roll around, even though we are many years down this road of grief. Why do I feel the need to broadcast it? Perhaps it's that I often feel a mass of pressure building up inside me, a load of sadness that needs an outlet. I feel the need for the world to know that my missing Hope and Gabe has not come to an end, and opening the front door to scream out in pain doesn't quite seem appropriate. I long for a connection with other people willing to acknowledge and share in my sorrow in some small way, even if it is simply the click of a "like" button. When people take this small step of entering into—instead of ignoring—these significant days, by simply commenting or "liking" a social media post or picture, it soothes some of the hurt. The truth is, the kindness of it usually brings me to tears as I think about that person at their computer or with their phone in hand remembering Hope or Gabe with me. It provides a release valve for the internal pressure.

> I look at the phone and wonder who to call to simply say, "I miss her today." I type the words via social media just to see her name in print and release a bit of those pent-up emotions. The support that I receive back is a balm for my aching heart.
>
> Devancy LeDrew[18]

When we've lost someone we love, we have a hard time understanding how the earth can keep spinning and people can keep doing the daily things of life since it seems that everything about our world has changed. We want the world to stop and take notice. That's what a blog post written by a grieving person is meant to do. That's what posting old photographs on the anniversary of someone's death is meant to do. It's a grieving person's invitation to the world to stop, at least for a moment, to remember and to be sad with her. It is grief in search of companionship.

Miss Manners says, "To express sympathy, it is essential to demonstrate that you are thinking about the person with whom you sympathize. A computer interface—the purpose of which is to reduce the time spent to an absolute minimum—will not convey this message convincingly."[19] And I agree that certainly our expression of sympathy shouldn't be limited to a text, an email, or a social media comment. But that is not to say that our electronic interaction with grieving people isn't meaningful or helpful. In fact, when grieving people are active on social media, this kind of engagement is one of the most significant ways you can enter into their sorrow. Of course, posting a message expressing sorrow on the Facebook page of someone who only rarely interacts on Facebook or other social media is probably not meaningful, and they likely will not see it in a timely way. But to neglect or refuse to comment on a post by a friend who has poured out his or her sadness on Facebook is to see their great sorrow and look the other way.

And, really, if you are someone who feels awkward approaching grieving people to speak about their loss, social media is a gift. You don't have to deal with initiating a conversation or figuring out how to end it. You don't have to make a phone call and risk catching the grieving at a time when they're not prepared to talk. You don't have to be afraid of saying the wrong thing under the pressure of the moment. You can carefully craft your words. But, really, it doesn't have to be anything laborious or long. You can leave a note on a Facebook page after the funeral that says, "I'm so grateful I got to be a part of celebrating your dad's life today." You can write about a brief memory of the deceased when something about their birthday or deathday is posted, something like, "Your mom always made the best chocolate chip cookies," or "I miss hearing him laugh." What moves me to tears and bonds me in unbreakable ways to people—some of whom are not necessarily close friends—is when they simply comment on a post about my children, "I remember." Or even better, "I will never forget."

One of the very best gifts you can give someone who is grieving is photos of the deceased. Whenever you discover a picture in your photo files that includes someone who has died, be sure you don't keep it to yourself. Posting the picture on Facebook not only gives their family and friends the joy of the newly recovered memory; it also creates a shared experience as others enter into the memory through their comments.

People often say to those who are grieving, "Call me if you need anything." That's what a social media post is—a call to let you know what they need. And what they desperately need is to speak that person's name by typing in the letters and seeing it on the page. They need to hear the dings and see the names appear of those who respond, assuring them they are not forgotten. They're telling you that they need a way to release all the pressure that has built up inside. They're "calling" you to tell you that the *anything* they need is for you to miss, along with them, the person who died so they won't feel so alone. Your online acknowledgment, by pressing the "like" button, is the balm, the *anything*, they really need.

Now, I know what you're thinking. You're thinking that it is a little creepy to "like" a post about someone's death. Let's just agree that the button may be awkwardly named for this particular purpose. Fortunately the folks at Facebook have supplied us with a number of new options besides just the thumbs-up sign. Now you can respond with a heart or a tear. However you acknowledge what has been posted by the person in pain, it will be a real encouragement.

> I find that I still want to talk about her and her death a lot. More than people want me to, or so I assume. It's the most life-altering thing I've experienced for bad as well as good, grace-filled, redeeming reasons. When people speak her name, acknowledge her existence, it reminds me that she was here, that she mattered, and that I lived through losing her because of Jesus! A "like" from someone means, "I'm still here, I care, and I want to hear you talk about your daughter and your journey."
>
> Michelle Smith, Arizona

> One of the first things I did after coming home without my son was to craft a Facebook announcement. I was desperate for community. I needed to be lifted up; I wanted to share my burden. Some of the first readers were my friends in other countries, so even in the middle of the night people were reaching out and crying out for us. All through the next day, the first full day without him, I listened for the alert chime from my computer every time someone wrote something, shared

something, or "liked." I didn't have the wherewithal for much that day, but I remember fondly the simple gift of community with every silent word, thought, picture, tear, and prayer that was shared socially. I didn't feel alone; despite the depth of my emptiness, I never felt alone. Social media has been a tremendous blessing in my grief.

Kristin Engel, Omaha, Nebraska

Facebook has given me a place to vent and for others to encourage me. A "like" lets me know that they understand as much as they can.

Tim Morrison, Cincinnati, Ohio

Somehow the comments and "likes" relieve some loneliness, buoy us up in our faith, and help us to continue to be honest and authentic about our sadness as well as our continued joy in parenting our three living children.

Jodi Blick, Omaha, Nebraska

When someone "likes" when I share my pain, I take that as a way of them expressing their virtual presence when they are not able to be with me in person.

Geoff Shive, Chicago, Illinois

Through Facebook we were able to share our pain with our loved ones despite the thousands of miles that separated us. Will would sit and read Facebook messages to me while I lay in bed trying to survive.

Etta Shehee, Tororo, Uganda

Maybe you think what they've shared is too private or precious to comment on. Maybe you think you are not close enough to the person posting to intrude. But the reason they posted it is that the pain of keeping it private has become too much to bear, and they want and need others to enter in. The very fact that you are not in their close circle of friends and yet chose to enter in makes your comment all the more meaningful. So enter in.

> Sometimes I feel like I am wearing out my nearest and dearest. But there are a handful of people who I know will always show they care by acknowledging an update about my losses as well as my joys. What surprises me is that oftentimes these aren't people I would have thought I was that close to outside of Facebook. Some I haven't seen in years. Yet Facebook allows us to connect, and it means a lot to me that the lives of my two children touched their hearts. I am sure my motives are not always pure in using social media. And it's a real battle. Yet it does offer a unique way of connecting with the most unexpected people over some of the most poignant points of life.
>
> Susanna Sanlon, Tunbridge Wells, UK

As I write to encourage you to persist in interacting online, I also think about what all of the blogs and posts about death and grief must be like for you. Perhaps you feel, at times, like so much is being constantly required of you in reading and commenting on every agonized post, admiring and entering into every photo memory, accepting or rejecting every invitation to participate in a memorializing or fundraising event. Surely it can begin to feel like a burden. Perhaps you've begun to wonder if someone's grief is bordering on obsession, and if commenting or "liking" is just feeding the monster of a seemingly bottomless pit of need for attention and sympathy. Certainly it can be hard to know exactly how and how much to respond and interact online with people about their loss.

Here's what you need to know: grieving people notice when

you frequently comment or acknowledge any and every kind of other status but go silent when they post about their loved one and loss. Your silence sounds like disapproval and perhaps even disgust and creates distance that is difficult to overcome. It feels to the hurting that you wish they would move on and stop talking about it.

Maybe your aversion to acknowledging their painful post is that you think they've posted enough about it. They seem obsessed with it or overly needy. Perhaps you are tempted to delete these status updates from your newsfeed because it seems their grief is all they ever post about these days, and, frankly, you're tired of it and don't want to encourage the trend with your clicks. Perhaps you think they're simply fishing for sympathy or attention and are demanding more from you than you and the rest of the online world wants to give. That may be true. And maybe if you are a friend who has walked with them through the loss closely enough to earn a place to talk to them about it, you should have a conversation. But probably the best thing is to recognize the continual posting as an expression of intense pain and loneliness and to offer the comfort that only costs you a click, along with a prayer for healing.

But here's one more thing you have to know, even as I encourage electronic and online compassion and support: there is nothing like getting handwritten notes and cards in the mail. Nothing.

> I got many, many Facebook posts acknowledging my loss, and I certainly appreciated them, but I had so many friends (close friends) who let that suffice and didn't send a sympathy card. A Facebook post is nice, but a sympathy card with a handwritten note is so much more meaningful.
>
> Beth, Minnesota

6

Let's Talk about Talking about Heaven (and Hell)

I don't think I really gave that much thought to heaven before our daughter, Hope, was born. It seemed very far removed and remote, somewhat irrelevant to all the more vivid and interesting things going on in the arena that had captured my attention—life on earth. But then everything changed. I knew when I held Hope that soon she would become an inhabitant of heaven. It mattered more. After she died, I knew a piece of me was there.

Shortly after Hope died, I was in church singing a hymn I had sung all my life. I suppose I had never before really thought through what it meant when I sang, "O that with yonder sacred throng we at his feet may fall. / We'll join the everlasting song and crown him Lord of all." For the first time, I saw in my mind's eye a face I recognized in that yonder sacred throng. I began to sense and long for that reality more than ever before.

It only makes sense that many of the conversations we have with those grieving the death of someone they love turn to the topic of heaven. In fact, I have come to think that one of the gifts given to us in the death of someone we love is that we think more about eternal things. We are awakened to the reality that this life is not all there is.

Those who want to be good comforters to those who are grieving have to be prepared for conversations and interactions regarding heaven. And if we're going to bring some clarity to what can sometimes be very vague or thoroughly confused or merely sentimental conversations, we have to become clearer ourselves on what is deeply, reliably, and eternally true about heaven.

The first thing we need to be aware of as we interact with those who have lost someone they love is that heaven cannot be assumed.

Heaven Can't Be Assumed

For many people, perhaps even most people in our modern Western culture, heaven is understood as the place where everybody goes when they die—at least everybody who isn't a murderer or terrorist or a former guard at a concentration camp. Social convention suggests that regardless of what the deceased believed or lived, we comfort grieving people by saying things like, "Well at least he's in a better place," or we try to get everyone to smile by talking about what the deceased is doing in heaven even as he smiles down on the rest of us chumps who aren't there yet.

But while our culture assumes that most people—or at least all "good" people who die—go to heaven, that is not at all what the Bible teaches. The Bible makes clear that there is not one person who is good enough to enter into the holy presence of God (Rom. 3:9–20). No one will inhabit heaven because he was a good person or because his stack of good works is higher than bad works. What it comes down to for anyone and everyone is whether that person became joined to Christ by faith. Heaven will be populated by flagrant but forgiven sinners who chose, in this life, to put their confidence in Christ's righteousness, not their own, as well as those who were too young or did not have the mental capacity to choose.[20] Heaven will be filled with people who saw themselves as they really were—sinners who deserved nothing less than hell—who threw themselves on God's mercy and thereby received what they did not deserve: heaven.

When the very religious and highly moral Nicodemus came to Jesus and asked how he could have eternal life, Jesus told him, "You must be born again." Don't be too quick to load down that term with modern baggage. Jesus was telling Nicodemus that he was dead spiritually apart from a work of God that would bring him to life. Similarly, Paul writes in Ephesians, "And you were dead . . ." (Eph. 2:1). All of us, by nature of the fact that we are sons and daughters of Adam and Eve, are born into this world physically alive but spiritually dead. Most of us don't think of ourselves this way. If we think about our sin at all, we think of ourselves as a little bit sick with sin but not spiritually dead in sin.

How is it that we are made alive, born again? "But God, being rich in mercy, because of the great love with which he loved us, even when we were dead in our trespasses, *made us alive together with Christ. . . .* For by grace you have been saved through faith. And this is not your own doing; it is the gift of God, not a result of works, so that no one may boast" (Eph. 2:4, 8–9). A person who has been made alive together with Christ may die physically but will never die spiritually. The person who was dead and was made alive together with Christ is as likely to die as Christ is likely to die. And Christ will never die.

But of course we know that there are those who do not see their need to be made alive with Christ. And when those people die, the sorrow for those left behind is multiplied. We should not always assume that the grieving people we talk to are confident their loved one is in heaven enjoying the presence of God. Imagine yourself in that situation (or maybe you are actually in it). Imagine that you never saw any sign that the deceased had a desire to be joined to Christ by faith or perhaps that person flatly rejected or ridiculed the need for Christ. If someone were to bring up heaven and want to assure you that your loved one is there, it would create anxiety, not peace. It would add to your agony instead of giving you assurance.

So what should you say about the eternal destiny of someone who has died? Here is where we must tread lightly but truthfully as we seek to walk beside those who grieve. This is where we go back to where we started in chapter 1 with the principle of "let the grieving take the lead." If they initiate a conversation about their confidence or their concerns about their loved one's relationship with Christ, listen and celebrate their confidence or mourn with them over their concern.

Sometimes when we're talking with someone who is grieving, we are so desperate to provide comfort, we're willing to say things we think she wants to hear that aren't necessarily true. But as much as we want to provide comfort in the moment, we need to remember that anything we say that is not ultimately true will ultimately disappoint. While we don't have to say everything we deem to be true, we do want to refrain from compromising, twisting, or abandoning the truth found in the Scriptures regarding life beyond this life in the presence of God. We don't want to gut the gospel in order to give comfort in the moment.

There are times we are likely to hear grieving people refer to their deceased loved one as being in heaven, when everything we know about the deceased would lead us to think otherwise. We need not try to convince the grieving of our concerns. But neither are we obliged to agree with and affirm their assumptions. If we must speak in that context, we should offer what we know is true about God (i.e., that he is so good as to take all who belong to him to himself) rather than speculate on what we don't know about the person who died.

Other times we find ourselves listening to those who are agonized by the prospect that the person they care about may be separated from God for eternity. They may be desperately looking for evidence and affirmation that the deceased was genuinely joined to Christ by faith, when there was perhaps little to no evidence of it. In these situations, once again we need to stick to saying what we know is true. And there are some things we know are true that can bring a measure of comfort.

First, *none of us can ever know the full reality of the interior of another person's life or the state of another person's soul.* We can observe evidence, knowing that "out of the abundance of the heart [the] mouth speaks" (Luke 6:45). We can often see fruit of repentance and belief in the lives of others. But not always. Just because we don't see it doesn't mean it isn't there. The question is not whether there was a lot of fruit or just a little; the question is, was there *some* fruit or *zero* fruit? If a person has been made alive in Christ, there will be at least *some* fruit. For the thief on the cross hanging next to Jesus, there would have been little fruit of a life of faith. But there was not zero fruit. There, in the final hour of his life, his eyes were opened so that he saw his sin, recognized Jesus as the one who could save him from the eternal death he deserved, and called upon Jesus to save him. And that was enough. People don't have to jump through our hoops to have a genuine relationship with God through faith in Christ. God alone knows the names that are written in his Book of Life, the names of those who belong to him and cannot be snatched from him.

Second, *we know that God always does right.* God is the very definition of goodness. Sometimes we think we know what is good and right and question God because, from our limited human vantage point, unable to see the end from the beginning but only our little slice of life, his ways don't seem to line up with what we've defined as good or with what culture holds up as good or even moral. But God himself is the plumb line against which all goodness must be measured. When we say that God is righteous, we're saying God is right. He always does right. This means that there will never come a time when we look at what God has done and will not be able to say, "You were right." This means that God will always do right by us and by those we love.[21] This means that though we can't say for sure what God will do in regard to the eternal destiny of someone who has died, we can be sure that whatever he does will be right.

What we need, and what those we are comforting often

need, is the encouragement to rest in the confidence that we can trust God to do what is right. But surely, when we are fearful that the person who died was not savingly connected to Christ, there will be very deep pain that will add to the sense of loss. As comforters we don't want to try to "fix" this pain by making false assurances of faith on the part of the person who died. Instead, we must be willing to share this pain even as we pray that God will grant peace and joy in the midst of great sorrow. We must be willing to seek with those who are grieving to become more thoroughly convinced of God's sovereign wisdom and goodness.

The third thing we know that can bring a measure of comfort is that *God's very nature is that of mercy.* When God revealed himself to Moses, he described himself as "merciful and gracious, slow to anger, and abounding in steadfast love and faithfulness" (Ex. 34:6). David cried out to God to blot out his sins "according to [his] abundant mercy" (Ps. 51:1). Paul writes that God is "rich in mercy" (Eph. 2:4). In other words, God is not stingy in the mercy department. It is the essence of who he is to shower his mercy on those who look to him for it. He is a God who loves to save. So we find comfort and offer comfort to grieving people not by pointing to a person's worthiness of mercy but to a God who is merciful. We find rest not in a person's evidence of having been saved but in a God who loves to save.

Heaven Is the Place Where God Dwells

In addition to the broad assumption that pretty much everybody goes to heaven or at least people who haven't done anything *really bad* go to heaven, there is broad misunderstanding of what heaven really is. Now, the visitation line is *not* a place for a theological conversation. And we simply haven't earned the right to explore theological questions with many people we will interact with in grief, but we do want to grow in our clarity about these things so that we can be a source of clarity to those who are confused or misguided or have simply absorbed an understanding of eternal realities from movies, television, or modern cultural ideas rather than the Bible.

However, the Bible does not actually provide a great deal of detail about what awaits the believer immediately following death. At least not as much as most of us would like. In fact, though we often talk about going to heaven when we die, there is simply no Scripture passage that states it that way. The Bible does tell us that people who have put their faith in Christ can anticipate four important things immediately upon their death.

1) *We will be with Christ.* Heaven is the place where God dwells. This is the most important thing about heaven. More than that, it is what defines heaven. The resurrected, glorified, but still human Jesus resides now in heaven along with all God's holy angels and all those in Christ who have died. Those who belong to Christ enter into his presence in heaven immediately upon their death. There is no waiting period or proving ground beyond this life.

Paul wrote, "For to me to live is Christ, and to die is gain. If I am to live in the flesh, that means fruitful labor for me. Yet which I shall choose I cannot tell. I am hard pressed between the two. My desire is to depart and *be with Christ*" (Phil. 1:21–23). The thief on the cross beside Jesus said to him: "Jesus, remember me when you come into your kingdom."

And Jesus said to him, "Truly, I say to you, today you will be *with me* in Paradise" (Luke 23:42–43). This means that you can comfort those who lost someone who loved Jesus this way: "The one you love did not leave this life to enter into an uncaring nothingness, devoid of relationship. Right now, he is experiencing a closeness and communion with Christ that is richer than he ever experienced here on earth. And it is good. I know it is so hard that he is not here with you, but I am praying that you will find increasing comfort as it becomes more and more real to you that he is at rest in the presence of Christ."

2) *Being with Christ will be far better.* The apostle Paul, who was given a vision of the third heaven where Christ dwells (2 Cor. 12:2–4), describes it as "far better" than life here (Phil. 1:23). Being in the presence of Christ won't be boring. It will be thrilling and fulfilling beyond our ability to imagine now.

Of course, this is the truth that gets transformed into a cliché that when said to the grieving person sometimes offends rather than comforts, because it can come across like a dismissal of grief. In an article of reflections on his comforters following the death of his brother, missionary Paul Stock wrote:

> A group of people walked towards me and one woman took my hands. "So sorry to hear about your brother's passing, but we know he's in a better place," she said. *Better for whom? His wife? His children?* Another hugged me. "God likes to take the good people home to be with him," the person muttered. *So we're the rotten ones?* Again, "You'll see him again in heaven." *But what do I do now?* And again, "Maybe God was saving him from an even worse death."

How do you know? People cared and wanted to help, but I wished they would just give me a hug.[22]

We don't want to use the truth of heaven in a way that seems to dismiss sorrow. But we do want to have our attitudes and responses to grieving people shaped by this profound reality. So rather than "He's in a better place," you can assure those grieving a loved one, who knew Christ, this way: "The one you love is being comforted by the environment of heaven, by the inhabitants of heaven, by the beauty of heaven, and by the king of heaven [Luke 16:25]. He or she is completely comfortable, completely satisfied, completely at rest in a place that is far better. I know it doesn't feel better to you that he is there, but I'm praying that the Holy Spirit will comfort you with a growing sense of the joy he is experiencing there and the anticipation of one day sharing it with him."

3) *We will be away from the body.* Paul writes: "We know that while we are at home in the body we are away from the Lord, for we walk by faith, not by sight. Yes, we are of good courage, and we would rather be *away from the body* and at home with the Lord" (2 Cor. 5:6–8).

A newspaper reporter followed our son Gabriel's life over its short six months so that she could write a story after he died. And she was kind to send us a draft of her story before she published it. I should have noticed that she rarely took any notes over the six months she spent with us. When I finally read the story, I realized why. She was content to make up quotes for us! Most of them I lived with, but there was one I insisted she delete. She had me saying, when we were walking away from the hospital after Gabe's death, "Well, at least now his crooked feet are straight." I know I didn't say it, because I know it isn't true. Gabe's body is in the grave; he is *away from the body*, at least for now. One day, on Resurrection Day, he will have gloriously perfect feet. But not yet.

When we think about our loved ones in heaven, we don't know how to think of them apart from the bodies in which we knew them, so we tend to think of them with bodies in heaven. But that is not the reality. The bodies they had that failed them are not yet healed and whole, not yet glorified. Their bodies are in the grave or condensed into ashes. Their spirits or souls are with Christ, and for now they are away from the body.

This means that we can certainly comfort the grieving with the knowledge that the disease or deformity, the aging or injuries, that plagued the loved one's body does so no longer. All physical, emotional, relational, and mental suffering has ceased. Those who have died in Christ are awaiting the day when they will be given a resurrected, glorified body like Christ's resurrected, glorified body. The day is coming when he will "transform our lowly body to be like his glorious body, by the power that enables him even to subject all things to himself" (Phil. 3:21). We find and give comfort as we nurture anticipation of that day.

4) *Our spirits will be perfectly holy.* The writer of Hebrews speaks to believers who have come to Christ and to the "city of the living God, the heavenly Jerusalem" (Heb. 12:22). Gathered there are "the assembly of the firstborn who are enrolled in heaven" and "the spirits of the righteous made perfect" (Heb. 12:23). Sin cannot enter into the presence of God. And when we enter into the presence of God, all our sin will not only be forgiven; it will be gone for good. We will never sin again.

In Ephesians we read that God the Father chose us in Christ

before the foundation of the world "that we should be holy and blameless before him" (Eph. 1:4). As we take in and chew on truths like this, we realize that when any true child of God dies, part of God's purpose in choosing us is wondrously fulfilled. We are finally and fully holy and blameless before him. This means that when you are talking with someone plagued by regret in the wake of losing a loved one, you can assure her that the person she loves who has entered into the presence of Christ is not resentful or plagued by hurtful memories. He is enjoying perfect peace and rest. He sees more clearly the sufficiency of the grace of Jesus, which covers and cleanses all sin. He has been purified and perfected. He is holy and happy.

One book I've come across communicates like no other these truths about heaven and how they can make a difference to the grieving person—the only one I've bought in bulk to give to people—is *Grieving, Hope and Solace*. It is a beautiful book to give to someone in the midst of grief, written by Albert Martin following the death of his wife, Marilyn. He writes about the perfection enjoyed by those in heaven:

> I was privileged to track that initial work of grace flowering out into Marilyn's progressive sanctification over the course of 52 years. . . . However, all that God had done in her subsequent to her conversion at age 19 until her home-going at age 73 could be put in a spiritual thimble compared to the ocean of grace poured upon her and into her the moment she breathed her last. In an instant, her spirit was purged of every last vestige of remaining sin, and she was endowed with the moral perfection of Christ himself.[23]

There are many writers and preachers and teachers who presume to find in the Bible much more detail about our existence with Christ immediately after we die. But, as I mentioned above, the Bible actually tells us very little about the time when we are absent from the body and present with the Lord. This can be frustrating to those in the midst of grief who are often desperate to know where their loved one is and what he or she is doing and whether they are watching the events of earth. We sometimes want the Bible to tell us some things it just doesn't tell us. And we can let that frustrate us and disappoint us, or we can take hold of what the Bible does present in order that we might grieve as those who have hope.

Let's deal, however, with a couple more common misunderstandings about heaven.

Common Misunderstandings about Heaven

People do not become angels when they die. If you interact with people who lose children—especially infants or unborn children, there is lots of talk of them becoming angels. Of course, the deceased of every age are often spoken of as having become angels. But people do not become angels when they die. Angels are a created order just as humans are a created order. The writer of Hebrews tells us that angels are "ministering spirits sent out to serve for the sake of those who are to inherit salvation" (Heb. 1:14). No doubt God sends angels to serve and protect us, as Scripture indicates. But these angels were not, at one time, humans.

Likewise, people who have died are not now "taking care of us." Our loved ones are not charged with the responsibility for our care, nor are they given the ability to take care of us or communicate things to us after they die. We don't need our loved ones in heaven to take care of us, as if they could. We have a heavenly Father who loves and cares for us, an exalted Son who "upholds the universe by the word of his power" (Heb. 1:3). We have the Holy Spirit who "intercedes for us with groanings too deep for words" (Rom. 8:26). Our loved ones are in the presence of the triune God. They are at rest. "Blessed are the dead who die in the Lord from now on. . . . They may rest from their labors" (Rev. 14:13). They are not now responsible for our well-being, nor is their focus on this broken world.

So what do you say when people talk about the deceased becoming an angel or taking care of them? It depends on who it is and the situation you are in. Oftentimes we can let it go. We need not feel the need to correct every person who says this. But when we are pressed to get on board with this rhetoric, or when the error persists and we've earned the right to speak, we might gently offer a little pushback, asking a few probing questions rather than giving a lecture. We might say, "Do you really mean that she has become an angel, or do you perhaps mean that she is with the angels doing what both angels and redeemed humans do in heaven, which is worship Christ?" It is likely that those who say these things have never really thought it through.

It is interesting that we read in 1 Peter that angels "long to look" (1 Pet. 1:12) on the salvation and grace that humans uniquely experience. Evidently it is far more glorious to be a sinful human being who has been saved and made holy in heaven by Christ than to be an angel!

When people talk about a deceased person "watching over" or "taking care of" someone else who has died, we might say, "It is certainly sweet to think about them being together. But what is even sweeter is to know that they are in the presence of God. He has taken them to himself, and he is the one taking care of them until Resurrection Day."

> I did not appreciate people who said that my dad, mom, and brother are angels watching over me. They are not. God is the one watching over me.
>
> S. B. Salem, Arkansas

Living here on this earth, we are so earthly minded that we can tend to think that those in heaven continue to be absorbed by all the happenings of earth. Those in the midst of grief long to sense that the person they have shared so much life with on earth is still sharing it with them from a distance. They want to believe that the one they love can see the milestones, the joys, and even the struggles.

Of course, we don't really know about the veil that separates heaven and earth. Maybe those who have passed through the veil are able to see what is happening here and have the benefit of seeing it with a heavenly perspective. But I sometimes ask those grieving people who seem to be overly invested in their loved one's continued oversight and involvement in their lives if that is really what they would most want for the person who has died. Do they really want their loved ones to remain focused on the reality of how their death is bringing so much sorrow to those who love them? Or do they want them to be at peace, at rest, enjoying the perfection of heaven?

THE MOST IMPORTANT ASPECT OF HEAVEN TO UNDERSTAND

The Bible holds out a hope on which to set our hearts, a day to long for, a reality to remind each other of, in order to comfort each other. And it is not merely a spirit-with-no-body existence in the presence of God, which believers enter into when they die. While that will be wonderful, it is not all that God has planned. One day, Christ will return to earth. And when he comes, all who have died in Christ will come with him. They will be given resurrected bodies fit for living on a renewed and restored earth. So as we comfort grieving people, we want to help them set their sights on the day the Bible sets before us as our greatest hope, which is this:

**One day heaven will come down to earth
so that earth will become heaven.**

Does this sound strange to you? It did to me too at one point. I am someone who has been in church and studying the Bible for most of my life. While there has always been significant focus on going to heaven when we die, I'm not sure I ever heard a mention of the life to come in the new heavens and the new earth until quite recently. Maybe it was said but I just didn't hear it or grasp it. I knew we would be given resurrected bodies when Christ returns, but I never thought clearly about where we would live in those resurrected bodies and how that existence would be different from our "away from the body" existence in the presence of Christ immediately following death. But clearly resurrection is the aim toward which the story of the Bible is focused. Resurrection is the essence of biblical hope.

Paul wrote: "I am sure of this, that he who began a good work in you will bring it to completion *at the day of Jesus Christ*" (Phil. 1:6). The work that God began when he saved you will be complete on the day he returns to this earth and makes you fully glorious in body and soul.

Here is how Paul expresses his greatest desire: "That I may know him and the power of his resurrection, and may share his sufferings, becoming like him in his death, that by any means possible I may attain *the resurrection from the dead*" (Phil. 3:10–11). Notice that his desires are not wrapped up in going to heaven when he dies but in experiencing resurrection.

Elsewhere Paul writes, "But we do not want you to be uninformed, brothers, about those who are asleep, that you may not grieve as others do who have no hope" (1 Thess. 4:13). This passage draws a distinction between those who grieve with no hope and those who grieve with hope. And what is the nature or substance of the hope held out to us in this passage? What is it we are to set our hopes on that will bring us the comfort and encouragement we long for? "*The dead in Christ will rise first. Then we who are alive, who are left, will be caught up together with them in the clouds to meet the Lord in the air, and so we will always be with the Lord. Therefore encourage one another with these words*" (1 Thess. 4:16–18).

Notice that Paul did not command us to comfort and encourage one another with the truth that the spirits of Christians who have died are in heaven, although that is very true and precious—especially to the grieving person who is desperate to know where his loved one is right now. Paul commanded us to comfort one another with the truth of the resurrection yet to come. Surely this reality should impact the words we use as we seek to comfort those who are grieving the death of someone they love who died in Christ.

And to grasp the full picture, we must see that it is not just our dead and decayed bodies that are going to be transformed and renewed when Christ returns. The whole earth, the entire cosmos, is going to be remade, renewed, cleansed, and re-created. The New Testament tells us that the entire creation is, even now, groaning in anticipation of the day when this will happen. Paul writes in Romans 8:

> For the creation waits with eager longing for the revealing of the sons of God. For the creation was subjected to futility, not willingly, but because of him who subjected it, in hope that the creation itself will be set free from its bondage to corruption and obtain the freedom of the glory of the children of God. For we know that the whole creation has been groaning together in the pains of childbirth until now. And not only the creation, but we ourselves, who have the firstfruits of the Spirit, groan inwardly as we wait eagerly for adoption as sons, the redemption of our bodies. For in this hope we were saved. (Rom. 8:19–24)

We are being swept up into a much bigger salvation than just our individual lives. That passage in Romans helps us to understand the bigger picture. God's plan according to Ephesians 1:10 is, in "the fullness of time, to unite all things in him, things in heaven and things on earth." When the time is right, heaven is going to come to earth. In fact, on that day, earth will become heaven. This renewed earth will become the place that God will dwell with all those who have put their hope in him. To encourage us to place all our hopes in what God is bringing about, God gave the apostle John a vision of what is to come:

> Then I saw a new heaven and a new earth, for the first heaven and the first earth had passed away, and the sea was no more. And I saw the holy city, new Jerusalem, coming down out of heaven from God, prepared as a bride adorned

for her husband. And I heard a loud voice from the throne saying, "Behold, the dwelling place of God is with man. He will dwell with them, and they will be his people, and God himself will be with them as their God. He will wipe away every tear from their eyes, and death shall be no more, neither shall there be mourning, nor crying, nor pain anymore, for the former things have passed away." (Rev. 21:1–4)

Clearly, what the New Testament writers hold out to us to look forward to, long for, and encourage others to put their hope in is the day when Christ returns and the bodies of believers are resurrected and the whole creation is re-created. But perhaps you're wondering what difference this really makes, especially in terms of how we can offer comfort to the grieving. Following are five reasons we should encourage those who are grieving to plant their hopes in the soil of the new heaven and the new earth.

1) *Accepting what the Bible presents to us about our time away from the body equips us to reject false answers to those questions.* As I said earlier, when someone we love and have shared life with leaves this life and enters into heaven, we have a deep-seated longing to know what she is doing and what that new environment is like. Many people, not finding enough desired detail in Scripture, turn for insight, in their grief-fueled longing, to books written by people who claim to have died and gone to heaven and come back.

People sometimes say these stories encouraged their faith or the faith of someone they know. But they actually diminish biblical faith by elevating claims of a person's supernatural experience over the substance of the Scriptures. Most of these claims of seeing into heaven focus on earthbound concerns and stunted human desires that lack what the Bible describes as the heart of heaven—the glory of God, the Lamb who was slain on the throne of the universe. In embracing these stories, we're saying the Bible is simply not enough, that someone's mystical experience is needed to add to, verify, or "make real" what God has said. But saving faith is putting all our hopes in who God is and what God has said as revealed in the Bible. It is being confident of what we can't see (John 20:29; Heb. 11:1), not being convinced by something someone else supposedly saw.

As we interact with grieving people, we want to encourage them to take hold of what God has seen fit to tell us in the Scriptures about life in his presence after death and to ask him for the grace to let that be enough for now.

2) *Anything we grab hold of and put our hopes in that is not true, though it may bring us temporary comfort now, will eventually lead us to disappointment.* C. S. Lewis wrote in *Mere Christianity*, "Comfort is the one thing you cannot get by looking for it. If you look for truth, you may find comfort in the end: if you look for comfort you will not get either comfort or truth—only soft soap and wishful thinking to begin with and, in the end, despair."[24] So much of what other people say and what grieving people are tempted to grab hold of in the face of death is mere sentimentality or strange spirituality. Instead of taking hold of these things, we want to encourage grieving people to rely fully on the Scriptures and let the rock-solid truth revealed there be the ground underneath our unsteady feet and the anchor for our hopes.

3) *Nurturing our longing for resurrection soothes some of the agonies of death.* The lowest point of my life was putting

Hope's body in the grave and walking away. Everything about it felt wrong. That was in the heat of summer. Then came the cold of winter. I remember the October morning when heat came on for the first time that season. I awoke to the smell of burning dust from the heating system, and I could hardly bear it. The reality that Hope's body was deteriorating in the cold ground was agonizing to me.

People often say, "That is not her; that's just her body in the grave. She is in heaven." But they don't understand. I loved and cared for that body. I knew her and loved her in the context of that body. So it helps me to recognize that God values that body too. He's going to resurrect and renew it. While we aren't told everything we'd like to know about the resurrection bodies we will be given when Christ returns, evidently God intends to use the matter of our bodies that has long been buried in the ground, or ashes that have been spread on the sea or stored in a box, as the source material for resurrected bodies that will be fit for existence in the new heaven and the new earth. Once again, Albert Martin speaks to this:

> Up until Marilyn was diagnosed with cancer, we had spoken occasionally about the necessity of obtaining burial plots. Not until we were well into her six-year battle with cancer did we finally obtain those plots, though. And from the very beginning of our taking legal possession of them, Marilyn identified them as our "Resurrection Beds."
>
> I vividly remember kneeling by her bedside, just a few weeks before she died, and saying to her, "Sweetheart, when God is done with you in the day of resurrection, you will be so beautiful that I will not recognize you. God will have to introduce me to you."[25]

As we allow our hopes to be shaped by the Scripture's promises of resurrection, the promise that the bodies of those we loved and cared for will be raised, renewed, and glorified, will become more real and more precious to us. On that day, we will see one another with real, physical eyes, communicate with real, physical tongues, and embrace one another with real, physical arms. The glorious truth we have to comfort and cherish with those in the midst of grief is that the day Christ returns, they and their loved one who is in Christ will experience this resurrection together, and it will be glorious. No one will regret investing all their hope in resurrection.

4) *Life together in the new heavens and the new earth is the reality that the whole of the Bible is pointing toward, which means that this is the reality all of history has been headed toward.* This is the future God is preparing for us—a future reality that will be so grand and glorious that it will have been worth the cost of the death of his innocent Son, worth all the waiting for it to come about. Why would we want to settle for something less than the fullness and completeness of God's glorious plan for the future he is preparing for his own? As we grow in our understanding of God's grand plan, we stop making the Bible and the Christian life all about how we can tap into God to get the life we want, and instead we begin to see how we get to be a part of what God is doing in the world to bring about his plan to redeem all things. And that helps us to grow in our ability to trust his sovereign plan for our lives. Confidence in the future emboldens us to face anything in the present. It enlarges our expectations of the future and adjusts our unrealistic expectations of life in the here and now.

5) *God is worthy of being known as he truly is. His grand*

plans and purposes are worthy of being embraced as they truly are. We don't want to try to reshape God and his purposes to suit our small agendas and stunted desires. To anticipate the glories of the new heaven and the new earth is to have the mind of Christ. Having the mind of Christ is to long for what he has set before us to long for, not something halfway. The future he has prepared for us is better than what we can imagine or construct. It will be worth waiting for. It is worth longing for now.

Oftentimes it is not until someone they love dies that people do any serious contemplation of eternal realities. The death creates an open door for those equipped to bring the Scripture to bear on the questions and the assumptions and the longings that emerge in the wake of death. The hope of being in the presence of Christ upon death and then resurrected at the return of Christ to live forever with Christ is the most solid and dependable comfort you can offer to someone who is grieving. Its comfort will never fade or be proved false. Resurrection is the answer to all of our most agonized questions about life and death in this world.

So the reality that the deceased is in heaven can't be assumed, and we need to understand what heaven really is. But even when the grieving are confident that their deceased loved one is in heaven and desire that the realities of heaven shape and guide their grief, we need to be aware that heaven doesn't fix everything.

HEAVEN DOESN'T FIX EVERYTHING

One night about a month after my daughter died, I went out on our back patio and looked up at the stars and said through tears, "God, I know that Hope is in heaven with you, but it just feels so far away from me." The separation hurt. The memory of her suffering hurt. Anticipating the reality of a lifetime on this earth before I will see her again hurt. The reality of heaven was not enough to eliminate my deep sense of loss and longing to be with her.

One of the statements I wrote in my first book, *Holding on to Hope*, that grieving people have often told me they found meaningful is this: "Our culture wants to put the Band-Aid of heaven on the hurt of losing someone we love. Sometimes it seems like the people around us think that because we know the one we love is in heaven, we shouldn't be sad. But they don't understand how far away heaven feels, and how long the future seems as we see before us the years we have to spend on this earth before we see the one we love again."[26]

Sometimes grieving people are told that they shouldn't be sad, because the person they love is now in heaven. But such a remark ignores the deep pain and intense loneliness the grieving feel. There is room to be both deeply joyful that the deceased loved one is in the presence of God while also deeply sad that he or she is no longer sharing day-to-day life on this earth.

Please don't tell me that "God must have needed her more," or, "She's in a better place," or, "Well, you have lots of good memories." What I don't have is my baby girl, and there is a hole in my heart the size of Texas.

Rosi Braatz, Lakeville, Minnesota

I am a believer and will see my loved one again, but sometimes the temporary separation is almost unbearable. I want to hug him, hear his voice.

Pam, Pennsylvania

Finally, while it is a good thing to be able to comfort the grieving with anticipation of seeing the person they love again in heaven, we should also be sure to talk about the greatest joy that awaits us there.

HEAVEN'S GREATEST JOY

A couple of months after our son died, a music-industry friend called and asked David, Matt, and me to be in a music video. A band that was unknown at the time—MercyMe—had recorded a song that was starting to get significant radio airplay, and a video was being created to play behind the band's performance of the song at an upcoming awards show.

The producers invited a number of people who'd lost loved ones to come to an old house where the video would be shot. Each person was asked to bring a picture of their loved one. So David and Matt and I brought our two large portraits of Hope and Gabe and somberly looked into the camera to do our part. The song was "I Can Only Imagine."[27] We'd heard it just a time or two before then, not knowing that it would become a huge hit—and a huge blessing to many people. The song focuses on imagining what it will be like when we enter into the presence of Christ and see his face, wondering what we will feel and what we will do.

It was fun to be a part of the video, and I love the song. But the video has always represented to me our Christian culture's conflicted thoughts and feelings about heaven. While the words celebrate the joy and the focus of heaven as being the presence of Jesus, the visual images of the video suggested that our longing for heaven is perhaps more about seeing those we love who've gone before us than about seeing Christ.

In his book *A Grief Unveiled*, Gregory Floyd quotes his wife, Maureen, who said at one point after their son died, "I really want to go to heaven to see Johnny, but I'm struck that I want to go almost more to see him than to see Jesus."[28]

When I read that shortly after Hope died, I could relate. Suddenly I found myself longing for heaven. It seemed so real. Yet, if I was honest, it was not Jesus I was longing to see and enjoy most of all; it was Hope. It seemed a sad commentary on the inferior state of my love for Christ.

But I've come to think this longing reflects our inescapable humanity. Right now we know and love Jesus through a glass dimly, and we long for the day when we'll know him face-to-face. But when we lose a child or spouse or parent, we've lost someone we've seen with our eyes and touched with our hands and loved up close. And God is the one who made us to love each other deeply. Surely our longing to see those we love is a tool God can use to awaken us to himself. When someone we love is in heaven, it becomes more real; our yearning for heaven becomes more vivid. And to long for heaven is a gift of grace.

It is a wonderful thing to bring comfort to those who have lost a loved one in Christ with the assurance that they will one day see their loved one again. We can celebrate with them that this is not false hope. We can look them in the eye and assure them that the day is really coming. We can encourage them to think of the time of waiting for that day in light of eternity (which, according to Paul, makes this life seem "momentary," 2 Cor. 4:17). While the years may seem to stretch out before them in which they will have to wait to join the one they love in heaven, in light of eternity, it really won't be very long.

We can also pray with and for them that God would use

their desire to see the one they love to awaken them more fully to himself. In heaven we will not have to choose between focusing on the people we love and loving Jesus with our whole heart. The joy of heaven—in fact, what will make heaven *heaven*—will be that together with those we love, we will look to Jesus.

> One dear brother wrote to me: "She who will likely precede you into the immeasurable gain of the nearer presence of Christ will remain your helper, as she, by her being there, will serve as a strong cord to draw and keep your affections heavenward."
>
> Albert Martin[29]

7

A Few Quick Questions

(and Answers)

Following are some questions that often arise concerning how to comfort the grieving and my suggested answers.

1) There's a Bible verse I want to share. Should I?

It depends.

If you're interacting with someone who has no regard for or familiarity with the Bible, quoting Scripture may come across as uncaring, overly religious, and out of touch with his reality. He may sense that you are trying to preach away his pain.

But if you're interacting with someone who belongs to Christ, someone who knows deep down that his only hope in the midst of loss is found in Christ, even though he may be filled with doubts and questions in the moment, humbly and lovingly sharing the Scriptures is perhaps the greatest gift you can give.

Megan Jameson has friends who clearly know how to do

this. Here is the text of a couple of the beautifully written notes laden with Scripture that she received in the wake of her son's death:

> News of Evan's tragic death and the thought of your ongoing sadness move us greatly. We can't begin to understand your soul's grief at the loss of such a precious little life. The sheer thought of the heaviness of your sorrow makes us wonder how it's even possible for you to carry such weight. Then we remember that Jesus has "borne our griefs and carried our sorrows" (Isa. 53:4). We love you guys and are certainly grieving with you as you mourn the loss of Evan. We trust that the "Father of mercies and God of all comfort" will hold you and tend to you, and we pray that he will enlist many brothers and sisters to make his love tangible to you.

Beautiful. And from another friend of Megan's:

> This is certainly a season to sow in tears, but take heart, dear friends, for "those who sow in tears shall reap with shouts of joy!" Sow your seeds of faith and water them with your tears, knowing that you will come dancing and skipping with sheaves in hand (Psalm 126). Sorrow may last for the night, but joy comes in the morning. For the one who said, "Behold, I am making all things new," is the one who promised to wipe away every tear from your eyes, to banish death, and to put an end to all pain. Until then, we weep with you and pray for you.

Do you see what they did there? Instead of quoting Scripture *at* Megan, they wove it into their own thoughts and feelings. They expressed their own need for these rich truths and the confidence that the Word of God speaks clearly into Megan's loss. But they didn't seem to suggest that these truths of Scripture should make her loss hurt less in the here and now. There was no tone of telling her what she ought to do and what she ought to believe, but rather a shared sense of seeking to hold on to the truest truth in the universe when their world was being shaken. You get a sense, as you read the notes, that Megan's friends are standing beside her and her husband, lifting up their tired arms to take hold of Christ, not merely preaching at them or putting a scriptural Band-Aid on their deep hurt.

> I received cards from people that were honest in their own wrestling with what God had allowed in our lives. They used normal, everyday language, which meant it was from their hearts and not just rolled-out religious sentiments. The letters always came to a place that brought us to God and his promises and hope. We knew that as much as they could be, people were with us in it, taking us to God.
>
> Hannah Sadler, Manchester, UK

> For almost a year after the death of my son, a friend text-messaged me Scripture weekly, specifically to remind me of God's character and his promises in the midst of the greatest grief I've known to this point. I never expected it or knew when it was coming, but it always comforted me and helped me keep preaching the gospel to myself.
>
> Gabe deGarmeaux, Monaca, Pennsylvania

> After our son died, we had a couple of friends who texted us literally every single morning for six to seven months with a prayer, a stanza from a hymn, a comforting Bible verse, etc. We were so helped and encouraged by their faithfulness and com-

mitment to daily walk through those first few months with us, and we eagerly awaited their texts. They always made it clear that they didn't expect us to text back, which was also helpful.

Eric and Jodi Blick, Omaha, Nebraska

Good friends left a very nice message on our phone saying how they were praying for us and quoting Romans 8:35: Nothing can separate us from the love of God. I saved it and listened to it quite a few times.

Rachel Andrea, Cape Breton, Canada

I have had nine miscarriages in my young life. A dear friend of mine who has never experienced any type of infertility, miscarriage, or death in the immediate family would call me to sing psalms over the phone. Sometimes I would sing along, sometimes I would lie in my bed and cry while she sang. Once she even sang into my voicemail. Psalms like 40 or 63 really ministered to my heart, and then there were other days where something like 103 or a portion of 119 was the immense blessing. She knew she didn't have the words for me, but her habit was to pour the words of the Lord over me in my grief.

Melissa Joy, Elk, Washington

A while ago I got a message from my friend Starr Price, who had been at one of our Respite Retreats a few months earlier with her husband, Shane. Military personnel had just shown up at her door in Germany to notify her that Shane had died that day in San Antonio, Texas. And she was very alone. So I got on the private Facebook group for couples who have attended our retreat and asked them to respond with nothing other than a verse of Scripture which Starr could take hold of, and choose to believe in those difficult hours. I knew she didn't need expressions of sympathy or advice or promises of prayer in that moment. What she needed was the solidity of the Word of God to strengthen her for what lay ahead. Following are some of the verses fellow grievers posted for her that had become so meaningful to them in the midst of their own losses. It was so sweet, on this side of the Atlantic, to watch them appear minute by minute and then to see Starr go through and press "like" on every one. So if you're wondering what Scripture might be helpful to share with your grieving friend, here are some good ones. You will note that many are psalms—words God has given us to enable us to pour out our hearts back to him, especially in times of trouble.

Leslie Roe

"God is our refuge and strength, a very present help in trouble. Therefore we will not fear though the earth gives way, though the mountains be moved into the heart of the sea, though its waters roar and foam, though the mountains tremble at its swelling. There is a river whose streams make glad the city of God, the holy habitation of the Most High. God is in the midst of her; she shall not be moved; God will help her when morning dawns" (Psalm 46:1–5).

January 8, 2014 at 9:00pm · Like · 1

Lori Mullins Ennis

"Behold, I am with you always" (Matthew 28:20 HCSB).

January 8, 2014 at 9:07pm · Like · 1

Tara Storch

"What is impossible with man is possible with God" (Luke 18:27).

January 8, 2014 at 9:12pm · Like · 1

Lauren Byrne

Jesus said, "I have told you these things so that in me you may have peace. In the world you have trouble and suffering, but take courage—I have conquered the world" (John 16:33 NET).

January 8, 2014 at 9:17pm · Like · 1

Lesa Yancey Dwomick

"Blessed are those who mourn, for they will be comforted" (Matthew 5:4).

January 8, 2014 at 9:22pm · Like · 2

Tina Guidry Patterson

"I will not leave you as orphans; I will come to you. Before long, the world will not see me anymore, but you will see me. Because I live, you also will live" (John 14:18–19 NIV). Peace to you, you are not alone.

January 8, 2014 at 9:22pm · Like · 1

Jessica Jacobs

"Yea, though I walk through the valley of the shadow of death I will fear no evil: for thou art with me; thy rod and thy staff they comfort me" (Psalm 23:4 KJV).

January 8, 2014 at 9:25pm · Like · 2

Ted Dwomick

"For we know that when this earthly tent we live in is taken down (that is, when we die and leave this earthly body), we will have a house in heaven, an eternal body made for us by God himself and not by human hands" (2 Corinthians 5:1 NLT).

January 8, 2014 at 9:28pm · Like · 2

Jessica Terhune Anderson

"Likewise the Spirit helps us in our weakness. For we do not know what to pray for as we ought, but the Spirit himself intercedes for us with groanings too deep for words" (Romans 8:26).

January 8, 2014 at 9:32pm · Like · 3

Greg Sponberg

"The Lord is near to the brokenhearted and saves the crushed in spirit" (Psalm 34:18).

January 8, 2014 at 9:36pm · Like · 1

Dixie Taylor

"But he said to me, 'My grace is sufficient for you, for my power is made perfect in weakness'" (2 Corinthians 12:9).

January 8, 2014 at 9:45pm · Like · 2

Sarah Damaska

"But you, God, shield me on all sides; You ground my feet, you lift my head high; With all my might I shout up to God, His answers thunder from the holy mountain" (Psalm 3:3–4 MESSAGE).

January 8, 2014 at 10:12pm · Like · 1

Ruth Stel

"So do not fear, for I am with you; do not be dismayed, for I am your God. I will strengthen you and help you; I will uphold you with my righteous right hand" (Isaiah 41:10 NIV).

January 8, 2014 at 10:39pm · Like · 1

Melinda Potts Ross

"I cried unto the Lord with my voice, and he heard me out of his holy hill. Selah" (Psalm 3:4 KJV).

January 8, 2014 at 10:49pm · Like · 1

Landon Vick

"Trust in Him at all times, O people; Pour out your heart before Him; God is a refuge for us" (Psalm 62:8 NASB).

January 8, 2014 at 11:14pm · Like · 1

Kimberlee Patton

"I will faithfully reward my people for their suffering and make an everlasting covenant with them" (Isaiah 61:8 NLT).

January 8, 2014 at 11:28pm · Like · 1

Susan Shell Pruitt

"Come unto me, all ye that labour and are heavy laden, and I will give you rest. Take my yoke upon you, and learn of me, for I am meek and lowly in heart: and ye shall find rest unto your souls. For my yoke is easy, and my burden is light" (Matthew 11:28–30 KJV).

January 9, 2014 at 12:32am · Like · 2

Lindsay Tyson Jones

"The Lord is my rock and my fortress and my deliverer, My God, my rock, in whom I take refuge; My shield and the horn of my salvation, my stronghold" (Psalm 18:2).

January 9, 2014 at 4:07am · Like · 1

Eunice Bragan Galloway

"The LORD is near to the brokenhearted and saves the crushed in spirit" (Psalm 34:18).

January 9, 2014 at 4:19am · Like · 3

Tim Cutliff

"When Jesus therefore saw her weeping, . . . He was deeply moved in spirit and was troubled. . . . Jesus wept" (John 11:33, 35 NASB).

January 9, 2014 at 7:17am · Like · 1

Brian Brinkmann

"I lift my eyes toward the mountains.
        Where will my help come from?
My help comes from the LORD,
        the Maker of heaven and earth.

He will not allow your foot to slip;
        your Protector will not slumber.
Indeed, the Protector of Israel
        does not slumber or sleep.

The LORD protects you;
        the LORD is a shelter right by your side.
The sun will not strike you by day
        or the moon by night.

The LORD will protect you from all harm;
        He will protect your life.
The LORD will protect your coming and going
        both now and forever" (Psalm 121:1–8 HCSB).

January 9, 2014 at 8:01am · Like · 2

Michelle Goebel Smith

"Remember your word to your servant, for you have given me hope. My comfort in my suffering is this: Your promise preserves my life" (Psalm 119:49–50 NIV).

January 9, 2014 at 8:13am · Like · 1

Michelle Goebel Smith

"Have mercy on me, my God, have mercy on me, for in you I take refuge. I will take refuge in the shadow of your wings until the disaster has passed" (Psalm 57:1 NIV).

January 9, 2014 at 8:15am · Like · 1

Mary Elisabeth Cutliff

"The LORD also will be a stronghold for the oppressed, A stronghold in times of trouble; And those who know Your name will put their trust in You, For You, O Lord, have not forsaken those who seek You" (Psalm 9:9–10 NASB).

January 9, 2014 at 8:38am · Like · 1

Bevin Keene Tomlin

"Hear my cry, O God, listen to my prayer; from the end of the earth I call to you when my heart is faint. Lead me to the rock that is higher than I, for you have been my refuge, a strong tower against the enemy" (Psalm 61:1–3).

January 9, 2014 at 9:13am ·Like · 1

John Weddington

"But you, O GOD my Lord, deal on my behalf for your name's sake; because your steadfast love is good, deliver me! For I am poor and needy, and my heart is stricken within me. I am gone like a shadow at evening; I am shaken off like a locust. My knees are weak through fasting; my body has become gaunt, with no fat. I am an object of scorn to my accusers; when they see me, they wag their heads.

Help me, O Lᴏʀᴅ my God! Save me according to your steadfast love! Let them know that this is your hand; you, O Lᴏʀᴅ, have done it! Let them curse, but you will bless! They arise and are put to shame, but your servant will be glad! May my accusers be clothed with dishonor; may they be wrapped in their own shame as in a cloak!

With my mouth I will give great thanks to the Lᴏʀᴅ; I will praise him in the midst of the throng. For he stands at the right hand of the needy one, to save him from those who condemn his soul to death" (Psalm 109:21–31).

January 9, 2014 at 10:52am · Like · 1

LaDonna Vietti

"My hope is in you" (Psalm 39:7).

January 9, 2014 at 12:02pm · Like · 2

Dora Jenkins Perez

"Fear not, for I am with you; be not dismayed, for I am your God; I will strengthen you, I will help you, I will uphold you with my righteous right hand" (Isaiah 41:10).

January 9, 2014 at 12:21pm · Like · 3

Kim Eckels

"Lift up your eyes and look to the heavens" (Isaiah 40:26 NIV).

January 9, 2014 at 1:37pm · Like · 3

Tina Pickrell Zimmer-Leiker

"But those who hope in the Lᴏʀᴅ will renew their strength. They will soar on wings like eagles; they will run and not grow weary, they will walk and not be faint" (Isaiah 40:31 NIV).

January 9, 2014 at 5:36pm · Like · 1

Gillian Taaffe Peabody
"My flesh and my heart may fail, but God is the strength of my heart and my portion forever" (Psalm 73:26).
January 9, 2014 at 7:34pm · Like · 1

Starr Price
Thank you so much for the scriptures. I have not been able to sleep in the night time and I've been looking at them and reading them throughout the night thank you.
January 11, 2014 at 7:29am · Like · 3

2) It seems that my friend is depressed. Should I suggest a good doctor?

Maybe. Or maybe not.

What grieving people wish the people around them understood is that their sadness is not the problem. It makes perfect sense when a person loses someone they love and the life they shared together that they would be sad. And not just briefly; maybe not even manageably. To tell those working their way through grief that something must be wrong with them since they are still so sad suggests not only that they are doing this grief thing wrong but that the person who died really wasn't worth being this sad over, in this way, for this long.

> It's only been two weeks, but right now my grief is all consuming and exhausting. I am not depressed; I am grieving.
>
> Cynthia, Texas

Of course, sometimes grieving people really do need medical and psychological help. They need friends who are bold enough and caring enough and perhaps persistent enough to prod them to get the help they need. However, this suggestion should never be made in casual conversation as a "let me fix your problem" response to someone's deep sadness. Only friends and family who have come in close enough and stayed long enough to accurately assess the situation have the right to make this suggestion.

Such intervention can be done only by friends who recognize that there's a difference between being sad and being depressed. Feeling really sad is an appropriate, normal response to loss. Depression is a clinical diagnosis, a very real physical condition that can certainly be triggered by sadness, is marked by sadness, and is certainly intensified by loss. But depression isn't the same thing as sadness.

According to my friend Dr. Richard Shelton, who is Charles Byron Ireland professor, vice chair for research, and head of the newly formed Mood Disorders Research Center at the University of Alabama at Birmingham School of Medicine:

> In normal grief we would expect to see gradual improvement over time as the grief becomes less of a preoccupation. Within a few months the person with normal grief is sleeping and eating normally even though he or she may still be very sad. Talking to a grief counselor, a psychologist, a good friend, a Stephen minister, a pastor, are effective ways to work through this grief.
>
> But this is very different from depression. When people are not only sad, but have sleep disturbances, appetite disturbances, low energy, fatigue, hopelessness, helplessness, suicidal thoughts—then we're seeing the signs of a physical illness called depression. We know there is a problem when people go from thoughts of wanting to be with the person

who died . . . to talking about how they might join that person in death; when they have lost more than seven percent of their body weight within four weeks; or when they don't really feel sad anymore but are numb or emotionless.

These physical symptoms—along with negative thinking associated with being depressed—indicate treatment is needed. When someone's day-to-day life is significantly impacted with no signs of improvement over time—they're not able to go back to work, not able to do anything around the house—they should be evaluated for depression. And where there is any question, I would always err on the side of treatment.

With depression, the issue is chemical, not spiritual. There are chemicals in the body that are changed. The proper medication can normalize these chemicals so that people can function better, feel better, think more clearly.[30]

Some of us, especially those of us who have had previous bouts with depression, can be significantly helped through grief by medication. What a gift we have in modern medications that can replace and strengthen the chemicals in our brain and body that have been diminished by bearing the losses of life in this broken world. Medication, in the short and long terms, can give us a leg up to work through, think through, and talk through the loss.

But what many of us need instead of a pill is a safe place to talk through our experience of the death of the person we love. We need a safe place to talk about all the ways we're experiencing that loss and all our fears about never feeling better. For many, getting to talk through these things in a one-on-one counseling setting can be really helpful. In the case of traumatic deaths, it is essential. But a small-group situation that brings grieving people into community with other grieving people, helping them not to feel so alone, giving them an appropriate setting for continuing to talk about the person who died, can be just as or perhaps even more helpful. Yet here's the thing: it is really intimidating to the grieving to think about visiting a group like GriefShare. They're afraid they'll feel awkward or be put on the spot or that the rest of the group will be weird or simply won't understand their loss. They know how miserable they are, and it doesn't sound pleasant to be around other people who are also miserable. So you might look up the information about various groups that meet in your area, provide it to your grieving friend, and then go one step further. Offer to go with her. And then go.

3) My grieving friend is really angry at God and convinced that God is fine with that. Is he?

The basis of anger toward a person is a belief that he or she has wronged us. And isn't anger against God essentially the same thing—an assault on his character, suggesting that he has wronged us? Aren't we saying in our anger: *You are not good; your promises cannot be trusted; you have not done right by me, or my loved one.* And isn't it arrogance on our part to, in a sense, say to God through our anger: *If I were running this world, I would do a much better job than you have.* Aren't we insulting the "depths of the riches and wisdom and knowledge of God" (Rom. 11:33) when we suggest that God's plan for history, which includes this time between the cross and consummation—when bodies still die, when there is not yet wholesale physical security, not yet pervasive, permanent healing—is simply not acceptable to us?

When we feel anger toward God, we need not hide it. In fact, we cannot hide it. The question is, will we give it free rein? Will we keep throwing logs on the fire of our anger? Will we turn away from God in our anger or toward him with our anger, asking him to reveal himself more clearly so that we can correct all our incorrect assumptions about his ways, his promises, and his purposes that have become the basis for justifying our anger toward him?

Am I saying we will never or should never feel anger? No. What I'm saying is that as we work through our feelings about what has happened, and as we inform our feelings by what we know to be true about God and how he works, we reject the temptation to sinfully turn our backs on God in anger. We correct all our incorrect assumptions about God that gave us any sense of justification in being angry with him.

So, as we walk through grief with someone who is angry, we allow him to express the anger without judgment or correction. At least for a while. We earn the right to push back a little or, more importantly, point to the Scriptures. We encourage him to pour out his anger to God even as he asks God to correct his thinking and change his feelings.

Many of us assume that while God intends to change our minds—the way we think—our feelings are just what they are. We don't anticipate that God's work of sanctification includes transforming our feelings. But it does. And in actuality the two things—thinking and feeling—are connected. Our feelings are based on what we believe most deeply and profoundly to be true.

So with our angry, grieving friend, we come alongside, offering to open up the Scriptures together and work through the hard parts, asking God to reveal to us what is true so that he might change how we think *and* how we feel, so that seemingly justified anger will give way to peace and rest.

4) MY GRIEVING FRIEND IS DESPERATE FOR A SIGN FROM GOD TO ASSURE HER THAT HER LOVED ONE IS IN HEAVEN. DOES HE DO THAT?

Grieving people often talk about signs they believe God has given them that they have interpreted as assurance that their loved one is safe in heaven, signs that God has not forgotten them, and that he has been and still is involved. Some talk about having vivid dreams that they are desperate to interpret and to follow because they are quite sure that God, or the person who died, is trying to tell them something through the dream. And who are we to say that God did not send a rainbow, a cloud formation in the sky, a dragonfly, a ladybug, a deer in the backyard, or a dream in the night to communicate his care for his own? We probably shouldn't. But that doesn't mean we endorse any and every interpretation of what our grieving friend considers to be a sign from God.

The problem with giving too much credence to these supposedly supernatural signs and the grieving person's interpretations of them is that they diminish the clear communication God has already given to us in regard to his promises and his presence. Unfortunately, these messages are often afforded much more authority than the Scriptures in what we will believe and what we will do.

We do not need a supernatural revelation crafted personally for us to know that heaven is real, that those who die and have been united to Christ by faith are in his presence, or that God's presence by his Spirit is in and around us when we so desperately need him. It's all there for us in his Word. The problem, as we noted earlier, is that we don't think what the Bible has to say is enough for us. We don't see it as a supernatural word personalized to us specifically about our loved one.

What grieving people need is not a supernatural sign or an extrabiblical word from God. What is needed most is the Word of God, which is "living and active, sharper than any two-edged sword, piercing to the division of soul and of spirit, of joints and of marrow, and discerning the thoughts and intentions of the heart" (Heb. 4:12). What is needed to fill the emptiness is the fullness of God's sure and certain Word.

So what should you say when someone tells you about a message she believes she has received from God? I wouldn't be in a rush to say it was not from God unless it contradicts the revealed word of God in the Scriptures. But I would gently encourage her to regularly be in the Bible where she can be sure that what she's reading is a word from God. Perhaps you can offer to begin reading Scripture together on a regular basis to hear God speaking in a way that you are sure is his voice.

5) MY GRIEVING FRIEND HAS READ A NUMBER OF BOOKS WRITTEN BY PEOPLE WHO CLAIM TO HAVE DIED AND GONE TO HEAVEN AND SAYS SHE FINDS COMFORT IN THEM. WHAT SHOULD I SAY ABOUT THAT?

Probably nothing, unless your opinion is invited. But when it is, be ready. Until then, gently challenge the book's claims with what the Scriptures say. And when you have the conversation, be sure to subject your desire for theological soundness to your desire to truly empathize with the desperation your friend feels to know what her deceased loved one is experiencing in the heavenly realm. To have shared so much of life and not be able to know about or share the life that person is experiencing now is so hard.

But if you are invited to give your thoughts, or if you are in a place of spiritual authority that would compel you to speak the truth regarding these books, you might suggest that there are only five testimonies of seeing into the realities of heaven that are wholly reliable. There is Isaiah, who saw the Lord high and lifted up, seated on a throne (Isaiah 6); Ezekiel, who was given a vision of the future new heavens and new earth that he describes as a garden-like city in the shape of a temple called "The Lord Is There" (Ezekiel 40–48); Stephen, who, before he was stoned by the people of Jerusalem "gazed into heaven and saw the glory of God, and Jesus standing at the right hand of God" and said, "Behold, I see the heavens opened, and the Son of Man standing at the right hand of God" (Acts 7:55–56); John, who saw the risen and glorified Jesus seated on the throne of the universe being worshiped by all the people of the earth, all the creatures of the earth, and all the angels of heaven (Revelation 1, 4); and the apostle Paul, who was caught up into the third heaven and "heard things that cannot be told, which man may not utter" (2 Cor. 12:1–7). Isn't it interesting that Paul, who wrote most of the New Testament, did not include details about what he saw in his personal guided tour of heaven and said, in fact, that it should not be talked about?

None of these biblical witnesses claims to have died and come back to life. None of these testimonies focuses on meetings with other people who have died. These witnesses are clearly captivated by God alone. We read that they fell on their faces as their eyes beheld the glory of God radiating from his being.

Of course, the Bible does tell us about some people who died and came back to life. Yet it doesn't see fit to record their testimony about the experience. Evidently it just isn't worthy of being presented to us as a foundation for faith. If it were, wouldn't there be a book of Lazarus in which he gives us a rundown on those four days in the grave before Jesus called him back to life (John 11)? Matthew tells us that when Jesus died, "many bodies of the saints who had fallen asleep were raised" (Matt. 27:52). Amazingly that's all we're told. If the testimonies of those who have died and gone to heaven and come back to life provided something of value to help us to put our faith in the promises of God, wouldn't the Gospels contain their testimonies?

As we interact with grieving people we want to encourage them to take hold of what God has seen fit to tell us about life in his presence after death and to ask him for the grace to let that be enough for now.

6) Sometimes it seems like my grieving friend doesn't really want to feel better but wants to stay as sad as she is now. What do I do?

First, you have to understand something profound about grief and grieving people. It is our grief that keeps us feeling close to the person who died. There is a sweetness to the misery in that when we are thinking about that person, shedding tears over the loss, it actually helps us to feel closer to him or her. And we really don't want that closeness to end. So there is a part of us that really has no interest in feeling better, no interest in thinking less or crying less or talking less about our loved one.

One of the most difficult things about working our way through grief is that the day comes when we have a clear choice to make. We have to choose whether we're going to continue to allow grief to have so much of a hold on us. We have to decide if we're going to continue to give so much of our time, energy, and emotion to our grief, or if we are ready to make a turn, to begin to invest more of ourselves in the living than we are investing in the dead, more in the future than the past, more in living life than mourning death.

And it is a very painful choice. To make the choice to think less, feel less, and invest less in our grief feels like a betrayal to the person who died. It isn't; but it feels like it is. Here we are, hoping that people around us will not forget our loved ones, and we are the ones considering thinking less about them, grieving less over them. It doesn't feel right.

This pivotal point comes at very different times for different people. It can't be rushed. They might not even have the insight about their own grief to recognize the choice that lies before them. So to be a friend in this takes great sensitivity. In fact, they may not be able to receive the nudge back to the land of the living from you if you haven't been in the valley of the shadow of death along with them. They're likely to be willing to receive it only from someone who has had a similar loss.

So be patiently understanding of this inner agony. Let them know you look forward to the day the grief does not have the hold over them that it does now, but that you're not rushing them toward that day. Perhaps remind them that their love for the deceased is not defined by their ongoing misery. To keep on living and to actually enjoy life are not betrayals. To keep on living is to take hold of the truth of the gospel and live in light of it. To feel good again is to receive the healing found in Christ. It is to experience now, in part, the perfect and complete healing to come in the presence of God.

7) I'M THE ONE WHO IS GRIEVING. HOW DO I RESPOND TO ALL THE PEOPLE WHO SAY AND DO SO MANY THINGS THAT SEEM TO ADD TO MY HURT INSTEAD OF SOOTHE IT?

First off, I have to say, I'm so sorry. I know it hurts. More than that—it's maddening.

We tend to think that people *ought to know* what to say and what to do as well as what not to say and what not to do. But *why is it* that we think people who have not been in our shoes should know what to say to us? Did you know what to say to people before this happened to you? Have you ever avoided someone who was hurting or grieving because you didn't know what to say?

When we ask ourselves these questions, most of us are humbled as we remember life before—before the loss that changed everything about our lives, before we knew how much it mattered that every person in our world at least acknowledge our loss. This realization serves to diffuse our simmering anger and indignation. It summons us to come down from our high horse of "people ought to" so that we can begin to forgive those who have disappointed and hurt us. It frees us to begin to extend a hand to those who are so afraid of doing or saying the wrong thing around us so that we can welcome them into our world of sorrow without such stringent expectations.

The truth is that most people are hoping to be helpful, trying to let us know they can relate in some small way to what we're going through. If we put ourselves in their shoes, we realize it's tough to know what to say to someone who's grieving. So we can be prickly and sensitive about the things people say to us that we wish they hadn't, setting very high hurdles for people around us to jump through with their words. Or we can choose to see their brains searching for a connection, their hearts wanting to show us they care—even though they may not have the words to express it well. We can extend a hand to help people around us overcome the hurdle of awkwardness.

Here's the real question for you: Are you going to allow your disappointment and the offense you've taken to become a barrier to the people around you who care about you but have stumbled in showing it in the way you would have hoped? Are you going to let the little slights or occasional avoidance fester so that they begin to take over your interactions with people around you even as they make your soul even sicker than it already is? Are you willing to begin to overlook the insensitivities of others rather than collect them, recite them, and refuse to forgive them?

Oh, how I pray you will ask God to begin to do a work in your heart to extend forgiveness to others for their stumbling and bumbling attempts to comfort you and their awkward avoidance of you and their offenses against you. How is that going to happen? It will happen only as your awareness grows of your own offenses toward God and the generous forgiveness that has been extended toward you. We think our reason for not forgiving people is that they don't deserve it. But then we realize that we are people who don't deserve to be forgiven. We are people who keep on committing the same offenses with barely a thought. And yet we are people who have been granted a generous forgiveness. Forgiven people forgive. Won't you allow the generous forgiveness that has been granted to you in Christ to overflow toward those around you who have hurt you so deeply?

Perhaps the opportunity will come your way to let others know how they might grow in their ability to help grieving people. If you will welcome the work of the Spirit now to generate the spiritual fruit of forgiveness, you'll be prepared to share with others not only how they might do better in the future but also how they have hurt you in the past. And you'll be able to do it without animus or ugliness. You'll be able to say it clearly and humbly in pursuit of reconciliation and relationship. Perhaps you'll want to give some people a copy of this book, not to rub in their great wrong toward you or nail them for their failures but as an invitation to share in your sorrow.

Conclusion

It has been so good of you to invest yourself in understanding how to be a good friend to people around you who are grieving by taking in all that is in this book. There's so much more I might like to say, but hopefully what is here has given you a heart and equipped you with better skills and a few choice words and ideas for being a balm of comfort to the grieving people in your world.

And I hope you won't mind if I leave you with a few more thoughts from people who responded to my survey—just a few more things to think about as we say good-bye—answers to the question, "What do you wish people understood about your grief?"

> Time does not heal. Time gives you perspective. Time gives you the ability to process, think, pray, and do your best to understand your emotions. There are moments that I hurt like it was hours after the accident, and there are times I can just bathe in those emotions without them dragging me down.
>
> Todd Storch, Coppell, Texas

> I wish people knew that I love to talk about her.
>
> Mary Ellen Ashworth, Fayetteville, Georgia

I wish people knew that grief makes me feel like an outsider, as if I am now viewing life through the window inside my house, while everyone else is frolicking outside in the warmth of the sunshine and green grass. Grief is burdensome and lonely, particularly when once again I am the only one in the room who is crying. It is often more poignant when I am in a room full of people, like on Sunday mornings. Any acknowledgment of my pain, and of my son himself, is welcomed, even needed, as it lifts my burden for one moment.

Megan Jameson, West Des Moines, Iowa

I wish people would talk to me more about my son. Yes, he had his troubles and most of our friends know this. But that wasn't all there was to him! He was kind, sensitive, and very funny. I want them to share our good memories with us.

Anonymous, Tampa, Florida

I lost my best friend when my husband died three years ago, and I don't expect to ever be the same. The pain seems unbearable at times. My grief is ever present and part of my new existence. I disguise it as I go about my daily task, work, and social activities. My appearance on the outside may be totally different from what I am feeling on the inside.

Claybra Selmon, Tampa, Florida

I wish people understood you never remind me of it. It's always on my mind, and I think about my son all the time. I may be getting on with my life, working and being busy with things, but I love when anyone brings up his name and says anything about him.

Rachel Andrea, Cape Breton, Canada

I wish people understood that it took time for our feelings to catch up with what we know to be true about God and his sov-

179

ereignty. We felt naked, vulnerable, and exposed, especially at church. People care there, almost too much. Perhaps we could answer a question or two in the hallway going from worship to Sunday school, but by the third person who inquired, we would need to escape. We found that if we slipped in just as church was starting, or left just before the last note, it was easier than all the normal greeting time we were used to.

Sharon Smith, Muncie, Indiana

I wish people understood that while I may not have a body cast on, and I may not be limping along barely able to stand, that is, in fact, my state. You can't see that I am completely broken, because it is inside.

Donna, Texas

I wish people understood that when you pass that one-year anniversary it does not always get easier. Our second year was less about the accident and more about saving our marriage. The second year was probably more difficult, especially because others had moved on.

Sharon Smith, Muncie, Indiana

I wish people understood that my loss and my hurt are so huge and so deep and so profound. I know I'm not the same person I used to be. I'm not as much fun to be with. But in many ways I am more authentic and more real than I've ever been.

Julie Jones, Branson, Missouri

Some days my grief is as bright and burning as the sun on a ninety-degree day. It hurts my eyes to face it straight on. At other times it is just like a dimming sunset. I am able to watch it slowly fade until the next day when it once again is burning bright on the horizon.

Melissa Spiceland, Vinton, Virginia

NOTES

1. Kenneth Haugk, *Don't Sing Songs to a Heavy Heart* (St. Louis, MO: Stephen Ministries, 2004), 58.
2. Nicholas Wolterstorff, *Lament for a Son* (Grand Rapids, MI: Eerdmans, 1987), 35.
3. http://www.christianitytoday.com/ct/2014/march-web-only/kay-warren-grieving-mental-illness-suicide-saddleback.html.
4. Wolterstorff, *Lament*, 34.
5. Gregory Floyd, *A Grief Unveiled* (Brewster, MA: Paraclete Press, 1999), 111–12.
6. David Brooks, "The Art of Presence," *New York Times*, January 20, 2014.
7. When a couple loses a child, they are usually told that the divorce rate for couples that lose a child is 70, 80, or 90 percent. This is a myth. It began with the publication of Harriet Schiff's *The Bereaved Parent* (New York: Crown, 1977), in which Schiff, a bereaved parent, seeking to make a point about the stress the death of a child puts on a marriage, stated that 90 percent of the marriages end in divorce. She has since said that she never meant for the statistic to be considered as a reliable scientific study number. Since then, many speakers and writers commonly quote statistics that range anywhere from 75 percent to 95 percent, with no real basis. According to a 1999 survey and affirmed in a 2006 survey conducted by Compassionate Friends, a support organization for parents who have lost children, couples that lose a child are not more likely to divorce. In the more recent study, only 16 percent of couples that had lost a child got divorced, far below the overall US divorce rate of about 52 percent. The reality is that the death of a child appears to draw bereaved parents together more than it pulls apart.
8. Wolterstorff, *Lament*, 14.
9. David Guthrie and Nancy Guthrie, *When Your Family's Lost a Loved One* (Carol Stream, IL: Tyndale, 2008), 8.
10. Luke Veldt, *Written in Tears* (Grand Rapids, MI: Discovery, 2010), 129.
11. For more information about Respite Retreat, go to www.nancyguthrie.com/respite-retreat.
12. Elizabeth W. D. Groves, *Grief Undone: A Journey with God and Cancer* (Greensboro, NC: New Growth Press, 2015), 184.
13. See https://www.takethemameal.com.
14. Floyd, *A Grief Unveiled*, 38.

15. Taken from an interview with Rachel published in Guthrie and Guthrie, *When Your Family's Lost a Loved One*, 129.
16. Groves, *Grief Undone*, 147.
17. Go to http://www.griefshare.org and enter your zip code.
18. http://www.witf.org/bereaved/2014/01/why-i-want-you-to-like-that-my-baby-died-supporting-grief-through-social-media.php.
19. http://www.washingtonpost.com/lifestyle/style/miss-manners-expressing-sympathy-online-may-come-off-as-insincere/2014/05/20/c0686810-dd23-11e3-b745-87d39690c5c0_story.html.
20. Several passages help us with the difficult question of the eternal destiny of unborn or infant children and those who don't have the mental capacity to put their faith in Christ. In John 9:35–41, Jesus is calling to the man he healed, who had been blind from birth, to believe in him. Then Jesus said, "For judgment I came into this world, that those who do not see may see, and those who see may become blind." The Pharisees, who had the Scriptures and had seen Jesus's miracles, overheard what Jesus said to the formerly blind man and asked if Jesus was suggesting that they were blind, and Jesus said, "If you were blind, you would have no guilt; but now that you say, 'We see,' your guilt remains." In other words, as John Piper said in a funeral for an infant, "If a person lacks the natural capacity to see the revelation of God's will or God's glory, then that person's sin would not remain. God would not bring the person into final judgment for not believing what he had no natural capacity to see" (John Piper, quoted in Matt Perman, "What Happens to Infants Who Die?," *Desiring God* website, January 23, 2006, http://www.desiringgod.org/articles/what-happens-to-infants-who-die). In Romans 1:20 Paul writes of those who have not heard the gospel but have the revelation of God's glory in nature, saying, "His invisible attributes, namely, his eternal power and divine nature, have been clearly perceived, ever since the creation of the world, in the things that have been made. So they are without excuse." This could lead us to conclude that a person who does not have the capacity to see "his eternal power and divine nature" would, at the final judgment, have an excuse. It's not that God will save infants and those lacking the capacity to understand the gospel because they are sinless, but rather because God will extend mercy.
21. The Scriptures teach that God is just, or right, in condemning those who refuse his grace and mercy to eternal hell (2 Thess. 1:6–9; Matt. 5:29–30; 10:28; 13:49–50; 18:8–9; 25:46; Rev. 14:9–11).
22. Paul Stock, "Reflections on the Life of Dale," *Evangelical Missions Quarterly* 42 (January 2006): 60–65; emphases added.
23. Albert N. Martin, *Grieving, Hope and Solace: When a Loved One Dies in Christ* (Adelphi, MD: Cruciform Press, 2011), 36.
24. C. S. Lewis, *Mere Christianity* (San Francisco: HarperSanFrancisco, 2002), 25.
25. Martin, *Grieving*, 82.
26. Nancy Guthrie, *Holding on to Hope: A Pathway through Suffering to the Heart of God* (Carol Stream, IL: Tyndale, 2002), 9.
27. You can view this MercyMe music video at https://www.youtube.com/watch?v=N_lrrq_opng.
28. Floyd, *A Grief Unveiled*, 80.
29. Martin, *Grieving*, 94.
30. Richard Shelton, quoted by Guthrie and Guthrie in, *When Your Family's Lost a Loved One*, 45–46.

Subject Index

183

Scripture Index

Scripture Index

Hold Fast to the Promises of God
in the Midst of Suffering

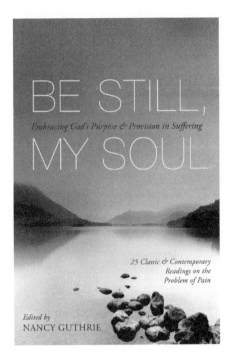

For more information, visit crossway.org.